Basic Skills You Need
Second Edition

H.M. Dobinson

Nelson

Contents

Abbreviations 3
Checking a bicycle 8
Checking a car 10
Coping in the kitchen and at home 14
The country we live in 18
Discounts 28
Europe, our neighbours 32
Filling in forms 34
Filling in an income tax form 42
Finding out by phone 46
Gardening 49
Giving directions 51
Handling timetables 53
The Highway Code 57
Holidays abroad 61
Holiday money 66
Layout 68
Layout on a typewriter 70
Locating in alphabetical order 72
Looking things up 74
Money sums 78
Percentages 84
Punctuation 91
Reading to children 95
Reading instructions 98
Reading the twenty-four hour clock 100
Sales literature and insurance 102
Seeing the doctor 106
Sickness in the family 109
Tidying up your handwriting 113
Trade unions 117
Using banks and cheques 123
Using a calculator 128
Using a dictionary 130
Visiting work places 133
Voting – for what? 134
The weather forecast 141
Weights and measures 145
What about fractions? 149
Will you get the job? 150
Wiring three-pin plugs 154
Work Experience 156
Writing a formal letter 162
Note to the teacher 165

Abbreviations

Lots of things are written down with just their first letters to save space. Sometimes the first two letters are used, or the first letter and one other.
These are standard abbreviations.

Where do these cars come from? (Spellings are given below)

1 F
2 I
3 B
4 GB
5 S
6 P
7 A
8 DK
9 N
10 CY
11 GR
12 L

We often refer to certain countries or groups of countries just by their initials. What do the abbreviations stand for?
You will find all the spellings you need in the list below.

America
Austria
Belgium
Britain
Community
Cyprus
Denmark
Economic
European
France
Great
Greece
Italy
Kingdom
Luxembourg
Nations
Norway
Portugal
Republics
Socialist
Soviet
States
Sweden
Union of
United

13 U.K.
14 U.N.
15 U.S.A.
16 U.S.S.R.
17 E.E.C.

WHAT'S THE REAL NAME?

Our English names for some countries are different from their real names. Car plates show the first letters of the real names. Use this panel of information to help you say what countries these cars come from.

España = Spain
Island = Iceland
Eire = Ireland
Deutschland = Germany
Nederland = Holland
Confederation Helvetia = Switzerland

18 CH
19 NL
20 IRL
21 E
22 D
23 IS

3

Tiny teasers

There are some very small countries in Europe, only the size of many a British city. Their cars have their own national identification letters. The panel tells you where they are.

Andorra is between France and Spain; Monaco is in the south of France; The Republic of San Marino is in north-east Italy; Vatican City is in Rome, in Italy; Furstentum Liechtenstein (the Principality of Liechtenstein) is between Switzerland and Austria.

Where do these cars come from?

24 RSM   25 AND   26 MC   27 FL   28 V

29 Trace the outline of the map of Europe on page 32, showing the coastline and the separate countries, and add the initials of each country, as used on the car identification plates, in the right places. Add the U.K. and U.S.S.R. as well.

POINTS ON THE COMPASS

People may expect you to be able to find the south-west corner of a map, or to identify the northern part of France. It is usual to print maps and compasses with the north at the top. Points half way between the four main directions combine both names – north-east is half way between north and east. Points nearer to one main direction than another use one name twice and the other once: north-north-east is nearer north than north-east is; east-north-east is nearer east.

The sun rises in or near the east; reaches the south at midday; and sets in the west. Time is measured as the sun passes the Greenwich observatory just outside London and this is called Greenwich Mean Time (G.M.T.). The sun reaches eastern England before it reaches Greenwich, and it reaches the west of Ireland 42 minutes later.

Using the information on the map and the scale below it, try to answer these questions:
If the sun rises at Greenwich at 6.00 a.m. G.M.T., approximately at what time does it rise:

1 on the east coast of Suffolk?
2 on the eastern borders of Wales?
3 in the west of Cornwall?
4 on the east coast of Ireland?
5 on the west coast of Ireland?
6 in eastern Scotland?
7 at Barra on the western Isles of Scotland?

Starting from Sheffield what town or place is to be found approximately:

8   170 miles S?
9   35 miles N?
10 55 miles W?
11 120 miles N?
12 200 miles W?
13 80 miles SE?
14 70 miles SW?
15 140 miles WNW?
16 200 miles WNW?
17 210 miles NNW?
18 50 miles NNE?
19 55 miles ENE?
20 340 miles NW?

4

OTHER COMMON ABBREVIATIONS

Use the drawings here, and the list of spellings below, as clues to help you work out the meanings of these other common abbreviations.

1	A.A.A.	10	B.R.	18	R.A.F.	26	s.a.e.
2	U.F.O.	11	B.R.S.	19	R.N.	27	p. + p.
3	V.I.P.	12	B.B.C	20	M.P.	28	a/c
4	R.S.P.C.A.	13	P.O.	21	T.U.C.	29	a.c.
5	S.R.N.	14	Km/h	22	J.P.	30	d.c.
6	N.H.S.	15	P.C.	23	B.A.	31	P.L.C.
7	F.A.	16	P.S.V.	24	B.Ed.	32	& Co. Ltd.
8	V.A.T.	17	N.A.T.O.	25	B.Sc.	33	M.E.P.
9	I.T.V.						

Spellings you may need

account	constable	member	registered
added	corporation	national	road
addressed	cruelty	navy	royal
air	current	north	science
alternating	direct	nurse	service
amateur	education	object	services
and	envelope	office	society
animals	European	organisation	stamped
arts	flying	packing	state
association	football	parliament	tax
athletics	force	peace	television
Atlantic	health	per	trades
authority	hour	person	treaty
bachelor	important	police	unidentified
British	independent	post	union
broadcasting	justice	prevention	value
company	kilometres	public	vehicle
congress	limited	rail	very

6

NOT OBVIOUS

The meanings of some abbreviations are not easy to work out. This is because they are abbreviations of words in another language. This panel gives what they mean.

&c. (or) etc. = et cetera = and so on
e.g. = for example
i.e = that is to say
q.v. = see the list below
A.D. = after the birth of Christ
B.C. = before the birth of Christ
p.a. = each year (per annum)
a.m. = morning
p.m. = afternoon or evening
ad lib. = without limit
pro tem. = for the time being
R.S.V.P. = please reply
No. = number
P.S. = post-script (added later)
c. = approximately (approx.)

Using the panel of information given here, write out these sentences in full, so that the meaning is quite clear.

1. Exhibit No. 17, a carving from 2 000 B.C., is removed from this showcase pro tem., and will be found among the art collection (i.e. carvings), q.v.
2. Come to our party 9.00 p.m. – 2.00 a.m. Fruit juice and mince pies ad lib. R.S.V.P.
3. Timemakers Company, established 1815 A.D., manufacturers of all time-keeping devices, e.g. clocks, watches &c., require a clerk, salary £6 500 p.a.

Checking a bicycle

Write some clear notes in your own words to show how you would know that your bicycle is fully roadworthy.
(Don't forget to check with Oily Jim in the pictures.)

1 Is the saddle the right height? How would you know?

2 Are the handlebars the right height? How do you know?

3 How well do your brakes need to work?

4 How would you know if your tyres are safe?

5 How do you know how hard to pump the tyres up?

6 How tight should the chain be?

7 Why do you need to check the spokes?

8 Are the front and back lights working and have you got a reflector?

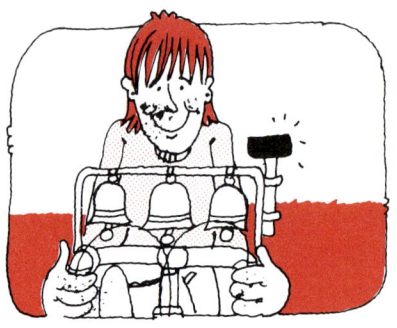

9 Have you got a bell or horn? You need one.

HOW TO MEND A PUNCTURE

Explain to someone else exactly how to mend a puncture. You can do this aloud or in writing. If you are doing it aloud, the other person could act it out, and you would lose a mark for everything you missed out, or did in the wrong order, or did not make plain. The drawings of Oily Jim at work will help you remember the right order. You might find the words in the price list below useful as well. A puncture kit usually contains patches, French chalk, rubber solution and sandpaper.

What is Oily Jim doing with his spanner and tyre lever?

Why does he need a bowl of water, French chalk, a patch and rubber solution?

How is he refitting the tyre?

DOING UP A BIKE

Peter and Penny both bought old bikes for rebuilding. These are the prices of the parts they needed in 1982. How much would it cost for the same parts these days?

PRICE LIST

Outer tyre, 26"	£3.85	Back light	2.69
Inner tube, 26"	£1.60	Brake cable	0.58
Rim tape	0.70	Handlebar grips (each)	0.60
Valves (each)	0.20	Bell	0.75
Valve caps (each)	0.07	Spokes (each)	0.08
Cotter pin	0.40	Pump	1.35
Chain	2.99	Puncture kit	0.60
Reflector	1.00	Sprocket	4.95
Saddle	3.45	Mudguards (each)	4.70
Front light	2.99	Brake blocks (each)	0.23

Peter's bike needed a new saddle, 18 spokes, a chain, 4 brake blocks, a brake cable, a reflector, and two valves.

Penny's bike needed two mudguards, 2 rim tapes, 2 inner tubes, 2 outer tubes, 2 valves, a cotter pin, 4 cable clips, and a saddle.

Checking a car

You don't have to be a mechanic to drive a car. However, if you take a car on the road, it is your responsibility to see that it is in working order.

This section deals with some of the things you need to check before taking the car out. They ought to be checked before every long journey, and also once a week even if no long journeys are made.

TYRE PRESSURE

You will need to know whether the tyres are radial or cross-ply, and what gauge they are – you will find details printed on the side of the tyre.

Measurements of pressure may be given in psi (pounds per square inch) or kg/cm² (kilogrammes per square centimetre). Most air pumps are marked with both scales. Use the right one!

Look up the manuals to see what the pressure should be in (a) any cars you have at home (b) friends' cars (c) the school minibus. Put your answers down like this:

	Make	Front tyres	Rear tyres
1 Cars at home:			
2 Friends' cars:			
3 Minibus:			

10

1 Make a job-list of the things that need to be done on the minibus that has been checked here, including the parts that you will need before it is fit to be taken on the road again.

2 Have two or three clean copies of the same checklist, and check over two or three cars (e.g. at home, friends, school minibus) to see if anything needs to be done to make them fully roadworthy.

Note the instructions here and on the next page about how to check the battery, oil, and tyre pressures.

DRIVER'S VEHICLE INSPECTION CHECKLIST

Date: May 30th
Make of vehicle: Ford Minibus   Registration number: MIN 805Z
Road Tax expires on: May 31st
Lights checked:

	Offside	Nearside
Headlight, beam	OK	OK
Headlight, dipped	OK	OK
Sidelight, front	OK	OK
Sidelight, rear	X	OK
Brakelights	OK	X
Indicators, front	OK	OK
Indicators, rear	OK	OK
Number plate light		X

TYRES

	Pressure	Tread	Cuts
Front offside	42 psi	5 mm	1, down to canvas
Front nearside	42 psi	5 mm	
Rear offside	44 psi	5 mm	nil
Rear nearside	39 psi	5 mm	
Spare	35 psi	12 mm	

Petrol: level in tank: E
Oil: level on dipstick: below 'refill' line
Radiator water level: expansion tank empty
Windscreen washer water level: OK
Wiper blades: both worn
Battery (each cell): all cells OK
Handbrake: OK
Footbrake: OK
Cleanliness of windows and mirrors: OK except nearside wing mirror cracked.

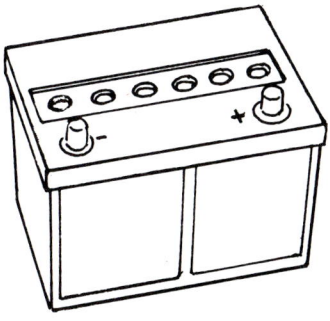

CAR BATTERIES

If you want to check a car's battery, take care not to let any dirt fall into the cells. Clean the cover before you open it. Top up with distilled water — tap water will not do in most towns. The water mixes at once with the acid in the battery; it should just cover the elements.

ANTIFREEZE

Manufacturer's guide
To keep the coolant unfrozen, it is recommended that antifreeze should be mixed in the following proportions;

Temperature down to:	−5° C	−10° C	−15° C	−20° C
Proportion:	1:4	1:3	1:2	1:2

How much antifreeze do they need in their cars?
1. Sean's van has a capacity of four litres of coolant, and he expects to meet temperatures down to −10° C in Coleraine.
2. Nicola's car has a capacity of ten pints of coolant, and she only expects temperatures down to −5°C where she lives in Hackney.
3. Errol's car has a capacity of twelve pints of coolant, and he expects to park it in temperatures down to −20° C when he is on a skiing holiday in Austria.
4. Sharon's car has a capacity of 6 litres of coolant, and she expects temperatures down to −15° C where she lives near Durham.

SPANNERS

Even without being a mechanic, you may find you need spanners for:
- tightening exhaust strap nuts and bolts
- tightening nuts and bolts holding extra fitments such as foglamps or membership badges
- tightening wing mirrors.

You may find these nuts are all different sizes. In many makes of car the nuts will be measured in imperial measures. Here are the measurements of some common sizes. Can you rank them in size order? (If you find it difficult, look at the note below).

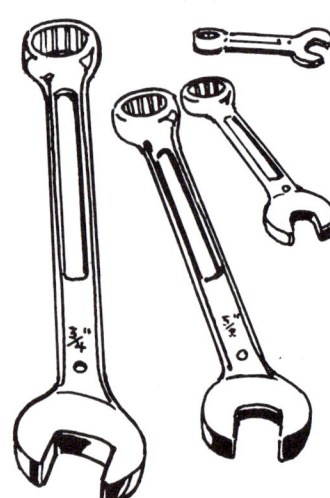

$\frac{7''}{8}$ 1'' $\frac{1''}{2}$ $\frac{3''}{8}$ $\frac{7''}{16}$ $\frac{9''}{16}$ $\frac{3''}{4}$

(Note: if you think of each of these sizes as a fraction with 16 as its base, it will be easy to compare them. If the fraction has 8 as the base, you need to multiply it by 2 (× 2) to change 8 into 16, and you must do the same to the top line of the fraction. If the base is 4, you need to multiply it by 4 (× 4) to change 4 into 16, and you must also multiply the top line by 4). (See also page 149. *What about fractions?*)

TAKE THE PART OF AN INSURANCE "LOSSER"

After an accident, the insurance company will send one of their staff, called a "losser", to assess the cost of damage done, and to see if the quotation given by the garage doing the repair is fair. (You should always wait until this has been done before letting anyone go ahead with repairs, in case the insurance company is not willing to pay so much).

Take the part of an insurance "losser", and put down details of what you can see needs to be done to this car:

1 Which body panels have been damaged?
2 Which windows have been broken?
3 Which wheel will need replacing?
4 Which door will need replacing?
5 Which lights will need replacing?
6 What else definitely needs repair?

CAR MANUALS

You can buy special manuals for all common makes of car and van used in Britain.
Use a car manual suitable for a car you have at home, or the school minibus, or a friend's car, and prepare notes or drawings to show you can recognise these parts:

1 carburettor
2 air filter
3 radiator expansion tank
4 radiator bottom hose and drainage tap

Prepare careful instructions to show you know how to do these jobs:

1 Change a wheel, using the correct jacking points and knowing how to remove hub-caps.
2 Fit a new fan belt.
3 Wash and polish all parts needing attention.
4 Check the oil level and top up if necessary.

Coping in the kitchen and at home

Kim:	Cor, I'll be glad to get in out of this rain!
Les:	Our own home! What a laugh!
Kim:	You sure they said it was furnished?
Les:	Yes, everything we need. They were even going to leave food in the fridge for us, and the telephone working.
Kim:	Did you remember to bring the key they sent?
Les:	Yes, here it is. All in order. Now let's move in.

     .. ..

Sounds are heard of washing, and running water.

     .. ..

Kim:	Les! I can't get this tap to stop running.
Les:	Let's see what a bit of muscle will do. That's funny. Not even I can stop it.
Kim:	Do you think the washer's gone? My uncle's a plumber. We could phone him up and ask him what to do.
Les:	You could ask him how to clear the drain at the same time. You can see it's blocked and we'll have a flood in a few minutes.
Kim:	O.K., but I don't know the code number for Waterlooville. Is there a code book there?
Les:	No, I'll have to phone Directory Enquiries. Is that 192?
Kim:	I think so. Give it a try. You can always dial 100 if you have problems.
Les:	Right, here goes.
Operator:	Directory Enquiries. Which town?
Les:	Waterlooville please.
Operator:	What name is it please?
Les:	Rivers, Mr Bill Rivers, but it's O.K., we know the number, except can you tell us the code please?
Operator:	Well, is it a four or five figure number, or a six figure number?
Les:	Kim, what's your uncle's number?
Kim:	28943. I always remember it as 'Two ate nine for three'.
Les:	28943. He's a plumber and we need to speak to him quickly you see. Water's flooding all over the floor.
Operator:	A plumber in Waterlooville, you don't say? Anyway, for five-figure numbers the code is 07014.
Les:	Thanks. 'Bye. O.K. Are you going to dial him?
Kim:	Right. 07014-28943. Takes ages! Les, go and get a bucket to put under that bowl. Then you can empty it in the loo.

     .. ..

Uncle:	The best thing you can do is start by turning off the stopcock. That's probably under the kitchen sink. Then you can just turn it on for a few minutes when you need water, and do the rest in the morning.
Kim:	Les! Turn off the stopcock under the sink.

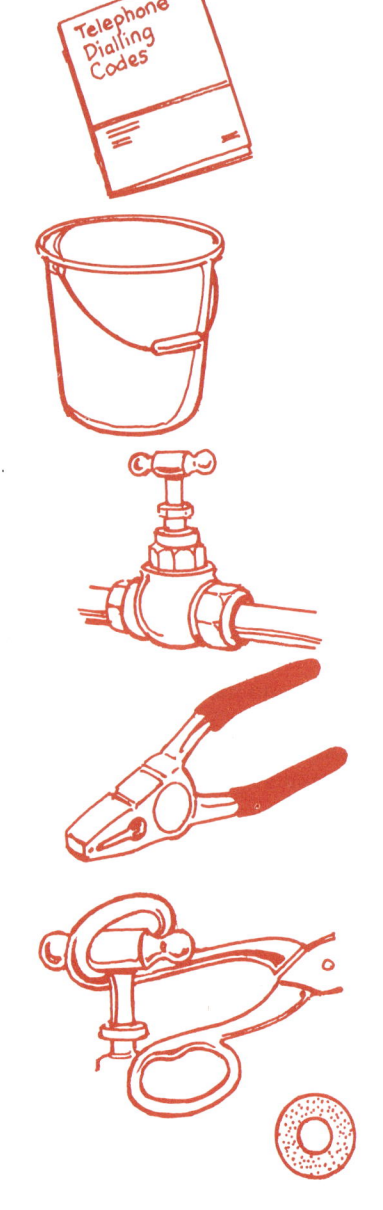

14

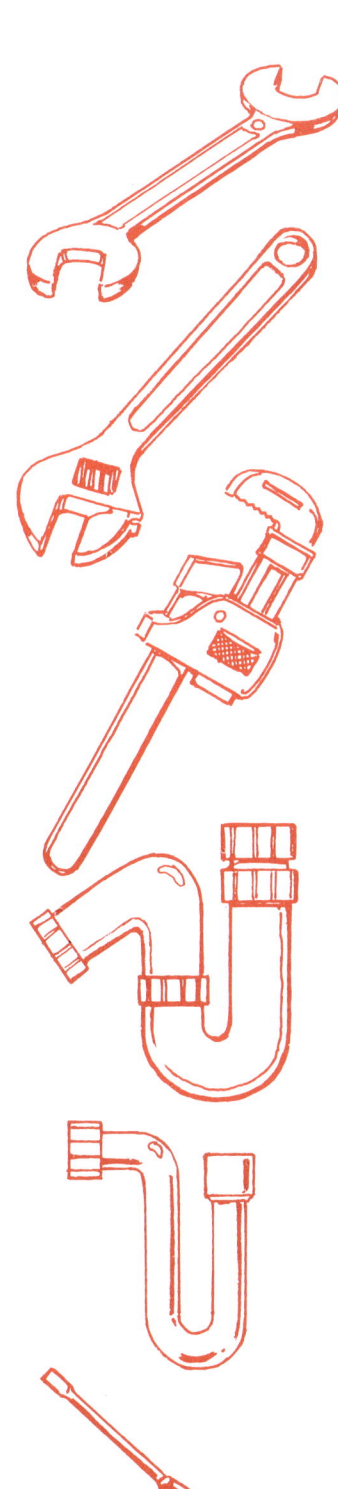

Les:	I've tried that, but it won't turn.
Kim:	He's tried that but it won't turn.
Uncle:	Chalked up, I expect. Get something to grip it with – pliers, or even the handle of the kitchen scissors.
Kim:	Try turning it with the handle of the kitchen scissors.
Les:	Which way does it go?
Kim:	He wants to know which way to turn it.
Uncle:	Same as all taps. Clockwise of course.
Kim:	Clockwise!
Les:	O.K. It's easy now. I was turning it the wrong way.
Uncle:	In the morning go and buy a half inch washer. Turn off the water at the stopcock, and then unscrew the top of the tap with a spanner. You would do best with an adjustable spanner and you may need a monkey wrench if it's badly chalked up.
Kim:	What have monkeys got to do with it?
Uncle:	Stop monkeying about. Tell Les a monkey wrench and leave it at that.
Kim:	Is that all?
Uncle:	And that blocked drain. Is the U-bend the old sort with metal pipes or the new plastic type?
Kim:	Les, is the U-bend metal or plastic?
Les:	Plastic.
Uncle:	That's easy then. You can probably unscrew it with your fingers and clean it out. You would need a spanner, pliers or screwdriver for the metal ones. Keep a bucket underneath while you do it. Good luck!
Kim:	Thanks, Uncle Bill. 'Bye. Les, go and make a cup of coffee will you? And what's in the fridge?
Les:	Tins of Coke, a loaf of bread, butter, jam, tomato soup. That's all.
Kim:	Oh boy! It'll keep us alive, but where are our proteins, minerals and vitamins?
Les:	Kim the dietician! Have you got an uncle we can phone up who runs a hotel at Barmouth?
Kim:	No, as a matter of fact he lives at Sandwich Bay.

.. ..

1 Make a list of the equipment and other things Kim and Les need, in the order in which they need them.
2 Describe aloud, or in writing, exactly what you would do when changing a washer or clearing a drain. Take a mark off for every mistake you make including leaving things out or doing them in the wrong order.
3 If you have a chance to practise doing these jobs, try your hand and see how you get on.

FEEDING WELL EVERY DAY

Kim, in the piece just before this, was complaining about the fact that there were no proteins, minerals, or vitamins in the food that was in the fridge.

The main sorts of food value we obtain when we eat are sugar, starch, fats, proteins, minerals and vitamins.

In our country we can easily have enough, or too much, sugar, starch, and fat every day, but if we are to keep really well, we also need enough proteins, minerals, and vitamins.

This chart gives details of foods that are good sources of proteins, vitamins and minerals.

NUTRITION CHART

Item	Proteins	Vitamins A	B(+)	C	D	E–K	Minerals	Notes
Beans (baked)	x							
Beans (green)	x						x	
Peanuts	x							High on calories
Other nuts	x							
Milk	x						x	
Lean meat	x							
Fish	x			x			x	
Carrots		x					x	
Butter		x						High on calories
Cheese	x		x					
Eggs	x		x					
Cabbage			x	x		x	x	
Oranges				x				
Vegetable oil						x		
Brown bread			x					

16

1. Plan your menus for a weekend to make sure that you have enough proteins, vitamins of all kinds, and minerals every day.
2. On the basis of this chart, what food elements might be missing from your own diet? Are these elements supplied by something else in your diet, or are you really short of them?
3. Try to find out from various reference books what other sorts of foods are good at supplying proteins, vitamins and minerals.
4. Which of these meals is cheaper at today's prices, and how big is the difference?
   Your total needs are:
   a Just over 2 lbs (1 kg) potatoes; just over 1 lb ($\frac{1}{2}$ kg) carrots; just over 1 lb ($\frac{1}{2}$ kg) of greens, or fresh peas if in season; just over $1\frac{1}{2}$ lbs ($\frac{3}{4}$ kg) fresh beef; just over 2 lbs (1 kg) fresh apples, pears, or plums; 1 pint (just over $\frac{1}{2}$ litre) milk, and a spoonful of custard powder and sugar.
   b 1 kg pack of frozen chips; some cooking oil; 2 medium tins of carrots; 1 large pack of freeze-dried peas; 2 tins of meat (corned beef or stewed steak); 2 standard size tins of plums; 1 tin of ready-made custard.
5. What can you find out about any loss of food value that may come from preserving food by canning, freezing, or about any synthetic chemicals (such as colourings, flavourings, and preservatives) that are added to such foods?

COOKING IN THE OPEN AIR

First make sure that you are allowed to make a fire in the place you have chosen. There may well be a barbecue hearth there already. If not, you should start by peeling back the turf and turning it upside down round the edge of your fire, ready to go back when you have finished.

Light the fire with plenty of thin brushwood, and then build it up to a good big fire. Do not start cooking until the really smoky stage is finished. You can then cook on the hot charcoal, which will be much better than on the open flame just after you have lit it.

1. What cooking utensils and supplies would you need for making a complete barbecue meal?
2. What are good things to cook for such a meal?
3. Make a list of places you could go to for a barbecue.

The country we live in

How much do you know about the United Kingdom apart from the area where you live?

If you meet some people you like, who come from a big city, but you don't know where it is, you can seem rude, and they will not be impressed with you. Or you might need to find one of the big cities on an outline map of the country while you are at work.

This section deals with information about Britain which can prove to be very useful.

It is difficult to give a good picture of a big city or a district in just a few words. The City of Cardiff is not big enough to appear in the list of big cities, but a wide range of types of work is found there.

SOME JOBS TO BE FOUND IN CARDIFF

iron works
steel works
rolling mills
foundries
patent fuel works
engine wagon works
motor component factories
enamel ware
hollow ware
paint works
port (oranges, timber)
furniture making
making bedding
making clothing
making footwear
making confectionery
making cigars
electrical goods
food products
building materials
administrative work (capital of Wales)
service industries (hospitals, shops, schools, taxis &c).

1 What jobs can be found in Cardiff and not in your own district or, if you live in Cardiff, what jobs can be found in Bristol but not in Cardiff?
2 What jobs are listed in the table of twelve biggest cities, but are not included in the list for Cardiff?
3 Which of the jobs in Cardiff are to do with metals?

THE TWELVE BIGGEST CITIES

Code on map	City	Population	Important jobs and products	Significant points
A	London	6 696 000	government, administration, docks	Westminster, 54 public parks
B	Birmingham	920 000	hardware, 1 500 trades	Bull Ring Shopping Centre
C	Glasgow	¨862 000	shipbuilding, engines	River Clyde
D	Liverpool	510 000⁻	docks	Mersey Tunnel
E	Sheffield	477 000	steel and tools	Peak District
F	Manchester	⁺⁺449 000⁻	textiles, food	Ship Canal
G	Leeds	⁺⁺449 000	metals, clothing	Headingley Cricket Ground
H	Edinburgh	¨450 000	printing	Castle
I	Belfast	¨410 000	shipbuilding	Parliament House, at Stormont
J	Bristol	388 000	aircraft	Avon Gorge
K	Coventry	314 000	cars	Cathedral
L	Bradford	281 000	textiles, micro-electronics	Yorks. Dales National Park

¨ = population figure quoted is previous to the 1981 census.
⁺⁺ = a large population lives just outside the City boundary.
⁻ = population falling rapidly.

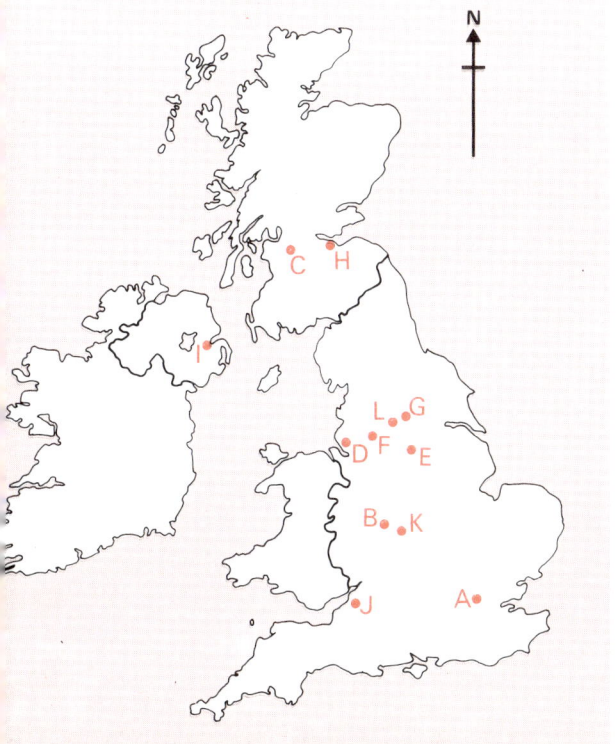

1 Trace the outline map of the British Isles, and mark on the places and names of the 12 biggest cities.
2 How many people altogether live in the eleven cities in the table, apart from London?
3 How many more people live in London than in all the other eleven cities put together?
4 What First and Second Division football teams are based in these twelve cities?
5 Try a 'Brain of Britain' quiz on the information given in this table.

SCANNING A TABLE OF FIGURES

When you see a table of figures like this list of 88 towns you don't expect to read it all. You expect to scan it – to run your eye over it for the things you want to find out. Try scanning this list to answer the questions given at the end of it.

#	Town	Population
1–12	See page 19.	
13	Leicester, Leicestershire	279 791
14	Cardiff, South Glamorgan	273 856
15	Nottingham, Nottinghamshire	271 080
16	Kingston upon Hull, Humberside	268 302
17	Wolverhampton, West Midlands	252 447
18	Stoke on Trent, Staffordshire	252 351
19	Plymouth, Devon	243 895
20	Derby, Derbyshire	215 736
21	Southampton, Hampshire	204 406
22	Sunderland, Tyne and Wear	196 152
23	Newcastle upon Tyne, Tyne and Wear	192 454 –
24	Dudley, West Midlands	187 228
25	Dundee, Tayside	¨181 842
26	Aberdeen, Grampian	¨181 548
27	Portsmouth, Hampshire	179 419
28	Walsall, West Midlands	178 909
29	Swansea, West Glamorgan	167 796
30	Luton, Bedfordshire	164 049
31	Northampton, Northamptonshire	156 848 +
32	Southend on Sea, Essex	156 683
33	West Bromwich, West Midlands	154 930
34	Warley, West Midlands	152 455
35	Basildon, Essex	152 301 +
36	Middlesbrough, Cleveland	149 770
37	Stockton on Tees, Cleveland	148 585
38	Blackpool, Lancashire	147 854
39	Bolton, Greater Manchester	146 722
40	Brighton, East Sussex	146 134
41	Bournemouth, Dorset	144 803
42	Preston, Lancashire	143 734
43	Stockport, Greater Manchester	136 496
44	Warrington, Cheshire	135 568
45	Thurrock, Essex	126 870
46	Birkenhead, Merseyside	123 907 –
47	Huddersfield, West Yorkshire	123 888
48	Reading, Berkshire	123 731
49	Norwich, Norfolk	122 270
50	Ipswich, Suffolk	120 447
51	Poole, Dorset	118 922 +
52	Havant and Waterloo, Hampshire	116 649
53	Torbay, Devon	115 582
54	Peterborough, Cambridgeshire	115 410 +
55	Solihull, West Midlands	111 541
56	Milton Keynes, Buckinghamshire	106 974 +
57	Newport, Gwent	105 374
58	Telford, Salop	103 786 +
59	York, North Yorkshire	99 787
60	St Helens, Merseyside	98 769
61	Oxford, Oxfordshire	98 521
62	Salford, Greater Manchester	98 024 –
63	Slough, Berkshire	97 008
64	Exeter, Devon	95 621
65	Oldham, Greater Manchester	95 467
66	Hartlepool, Cleveland	94 359
67	Gillingham, Kent	93 741
68	Paisley, Strathclyde	¨93 314
69	Rochdale, Greater Manchester	92 704
70	Grimsby, Humberside	92 147
71	Gloucester, Gloucestershire	92 133
72	Worthing, West Sussex	91 668
73	Swindon, Wiltshire	91 136
74	Cambridge, Cambridgeshire	90 440
75	Wallasey, Merseyside	90 057
76	Southport, Merseyside	89 745
77	Fareham, Hampshire	88 274
78	Blackburn, Lancashire	88 236 –
79	Halifax, West Yorkshire	87 488
80	Aldridge-Brownhills, West Midlands	87 219
81	South Shields, Tyne and Wear	87 203 –
82	Sutton Coldfield, West Midlands	86 494
83	Darlington, Durham	85 396
84	Redcar, Cleveland	84 931
85	Lisburn, Antrim	¨83 188
86	Londonderry, Co. Londonderry	¨82 862
87	Rotherham, South Yorkshire	81 988
88	Colchester, Essex	81 945
89	Rhondda, Mid Glamorgan	81 725
90	Doncaster, South Yorkshire	81 610
91	Woking, Surrey	81 358
92	Bath, Avon	79 965
93	Hemel Hempstead, Hertfordshire	79 695 +
94	Wigan, Greater Manchester	79 535
95	Harlow, Essex	79 276
96	Eastbourne, East Sussex	77 608
97	Gosport, Hampshire	77 276
98	Lincoln, Lincolnshire	76 660
99	Hastings, East Sussex	74 803
100	Worcester, Hereford and Worcester	74 790

Figures from the 1981 census except those marked ¨.
Towns where the population has been rising rapidly are marked + and those where it has been falling rapidly are marked –.
In some areas many people live just outside the town boundary.

Use the table of the twelve biggest cities as well as the list of towns to answer these questions:

1. Which British towns and cities have you
   (a) slept in (b) been shopping in (c) set foot in?
   How many people live in each of the towns you know?
2. How many people live in your town, or the town which is your local centre?
3. Which towns stand next to yours in this list in rank order of size? (Londoners: see the table of Boroughs on page 22 and answer for your Borough).
4. Which towns in this list are from these counties?
   (a) Cleveland (b) Merseyside (c) Greater Manchester
   (d) West Midlands (e) Warwickshire (f) Somerset
   (g) North Yorkshire (h) Powys?
5. Which towns in this list have names that end with
   (a) -ham (b) -ton (c) -port (d) -ford?
   (You should find six ending in -ham, thirteen ending in -ton, four ending in -port, and four ending in -ford.)
6. Which towns in the list have these numbers of people living in them?
   a Two hundred and seventy nine thousand seven hundred and ninety one.
   b Two hundred and seventy one thousand and eighty.
   c Ninety seven thousand and eight?
   d Ninety thousand and fifty seven?
   e Just over double the population of Gosport?
7. Which towns have been growing rapidly in recent years?
8. Which towns have been losing numbers rapidly in recent years?

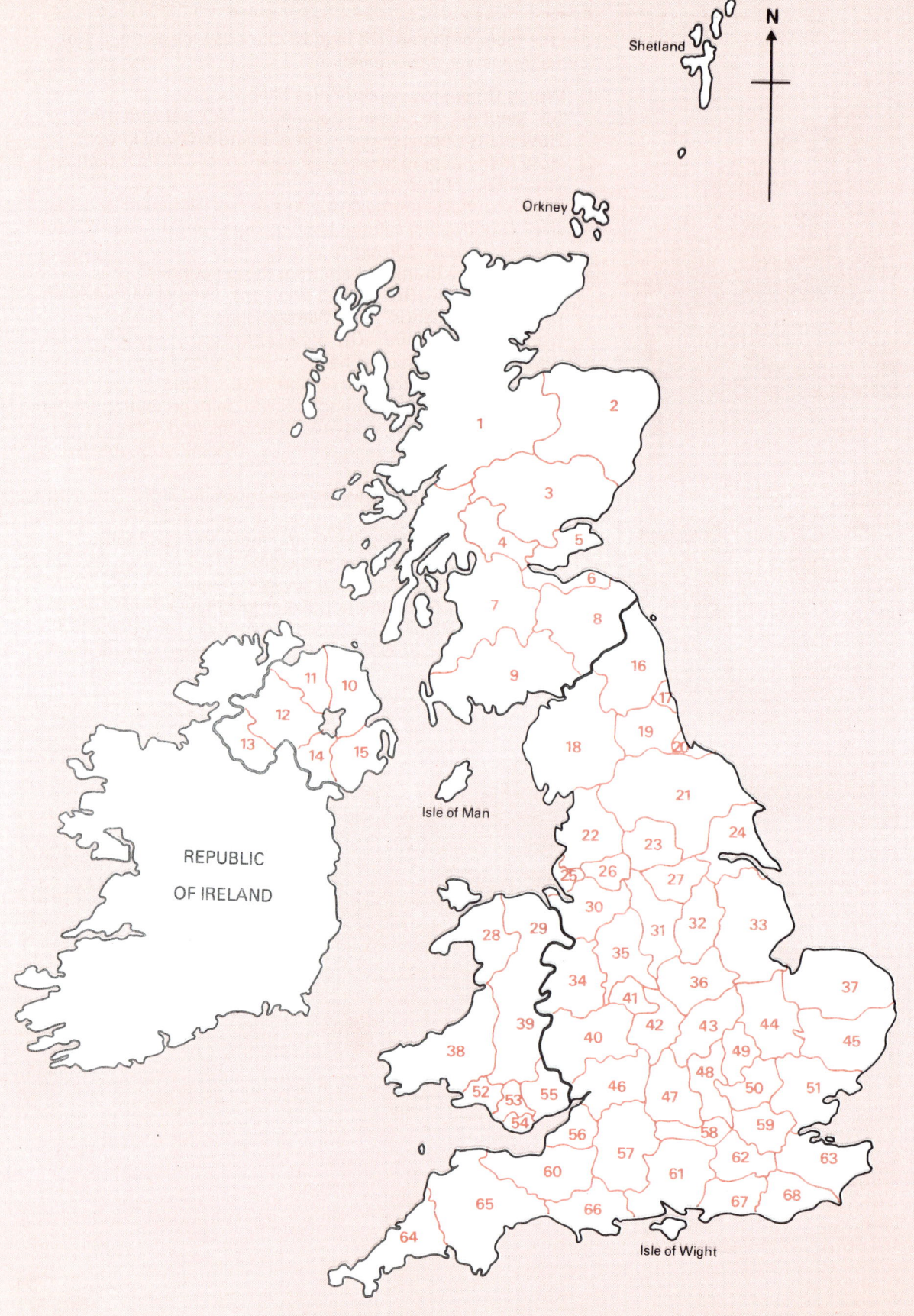

THE COUNTIES OF THE UNITED KINGDOM

Key to the map opposite

1	Highland	18	Cumbria	35	Staffordshire	52	W. Glamorgan
2	Grampian	19	Durham	36	Leicestershire	53	Mid Glamorgan
3	Tayside	20	Cleveland	37	Norfolk	54	S. Glamorgan
4	Central	21	North Yorkshire	38	Dyfed	55	Gwent
5	Fife	22	Lancashire	39	Powys	56	Avon
6	Lothian	23	West Yorkshire	40	Hereford & Worcester	57	Wiltshire
7	Strathclyde	24	Humberside	41	West Midlands	58	Berkshire
8	Borders	25	Merseyside	42	Warwickshire	59	Greater London
9	Dumfries & Galloway	26	Greater Manchester	43	Northampton	60	Somerset
10	Antrim	27	South Yorkshire	44	Cambridgeshire	61	Hampshire
11	Londonderry	28	Gwynedd	45	Suffolk	62	Surrey
12	Tyrone	29	Clwyd	46	Gloucestershire	63	Kent
13	Fermanagh	30	Cheshire	47	Oxfordshire	64	Cornwall
14	Armagh	31	Derbyshire	48	Buckinghamshire	65	Devon
15	Down	32	Nottinghamshire	49	Bedfordshire	66	Dorset
16	Northumberland	33	Lincolnshire	50	Hertfordshire	67	W. Sussex
17	Tyne & Wear	34	Salop	51	Essex	68	E. Sussex

1 Which county do you live in?
2 Which counties have borders that touch the one you live in?
3 Which are the largest counties (in area) in
  (a) Scotland (b) England (c) Wales?
4 Name one small (in area) county in Scotland, one small one in Wales, and four small ones in England.
5 Which counties have quite a lot of coastline on both their northern and southern borders?
6 Which other English counties have coastline on their northern borders?
7 Which counties in the north of England have coastline on their extreme borders?
8 Name 22 counties that cannot be reached directly from the sea.
9 On this scale, a circle of paper cut to the size of a 5p piece is roughly 80 miles on the map, and a circle cut to the size of a 10p piece is roughly 100 miles on the map.
  a Centring the circle on Tyne and Wear, what counties lie within 100 miles of Newcastle?
  b Centring the circle at Margate on the north-east corner of Kent, what counties lie within 100 miles?
  c Centring the circle at Gloucester on the north-east tip of the Severn Estuary, what counties lie within 80 miles?
10 a Placing the edge of the circle on the northern tip of Leicestershire, what county do you reach just 100 miles further north?
  b Placing the edge of the circle on the most westerly point of Hertfordshire, which two counties lie 80 miles further west?

23

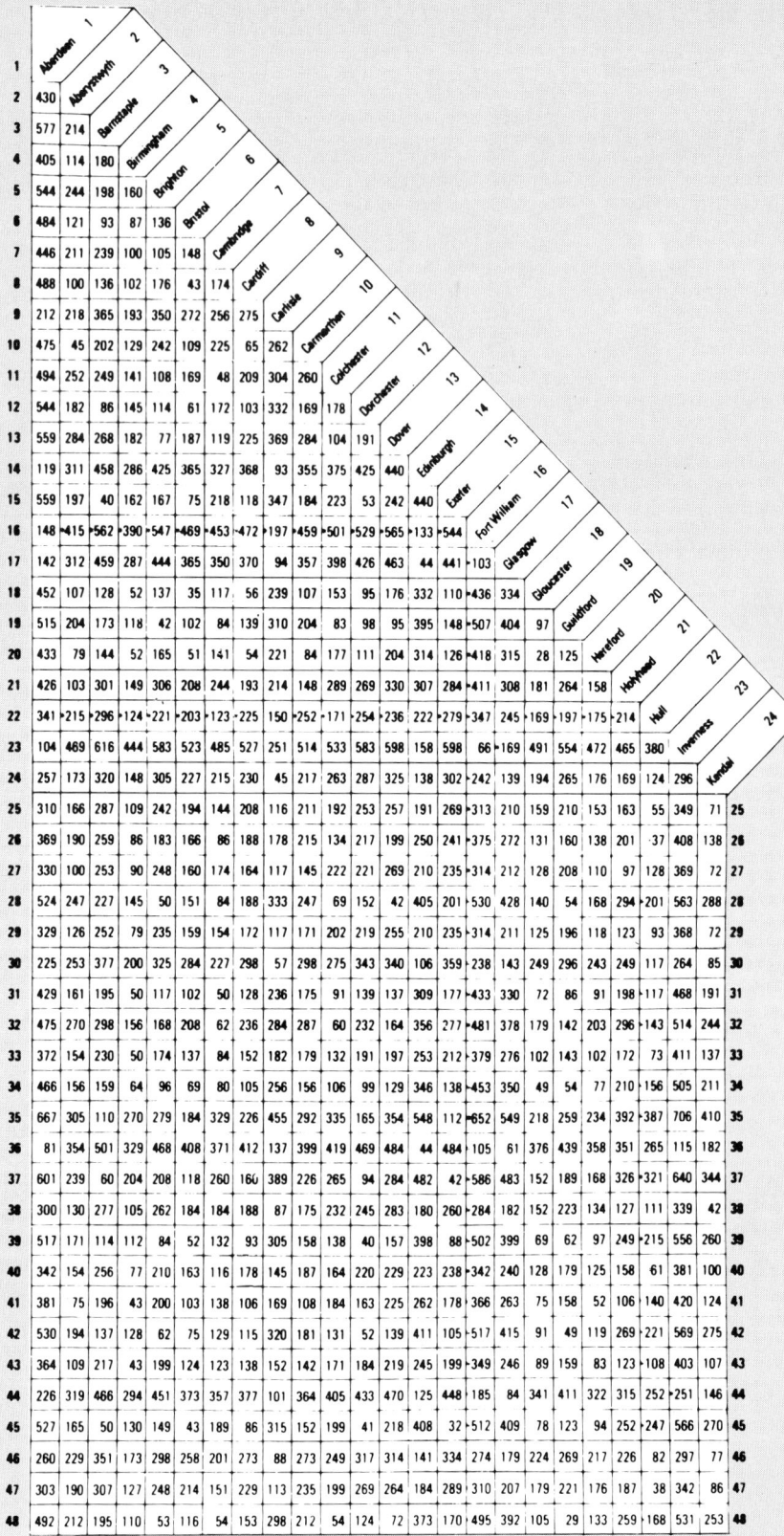

DISTANCE CALCULATOR

To use this distance calculator, you look at the name of the place where you begin, and the name of the place where you finish. Follow the lines from each, and the number in the square where the lines cross is the distance (in miles) between them.

How far is it from:
a Liverpool to Aberystwyth?
b Dover to Cambridge?
c Aberdeen to Inverness?
d Carlisle to Newcastle upon Tyne?
e Leeds to Penzance?
f Hull to York?
g Exeter to Perth?
h Bristol to Leeds?

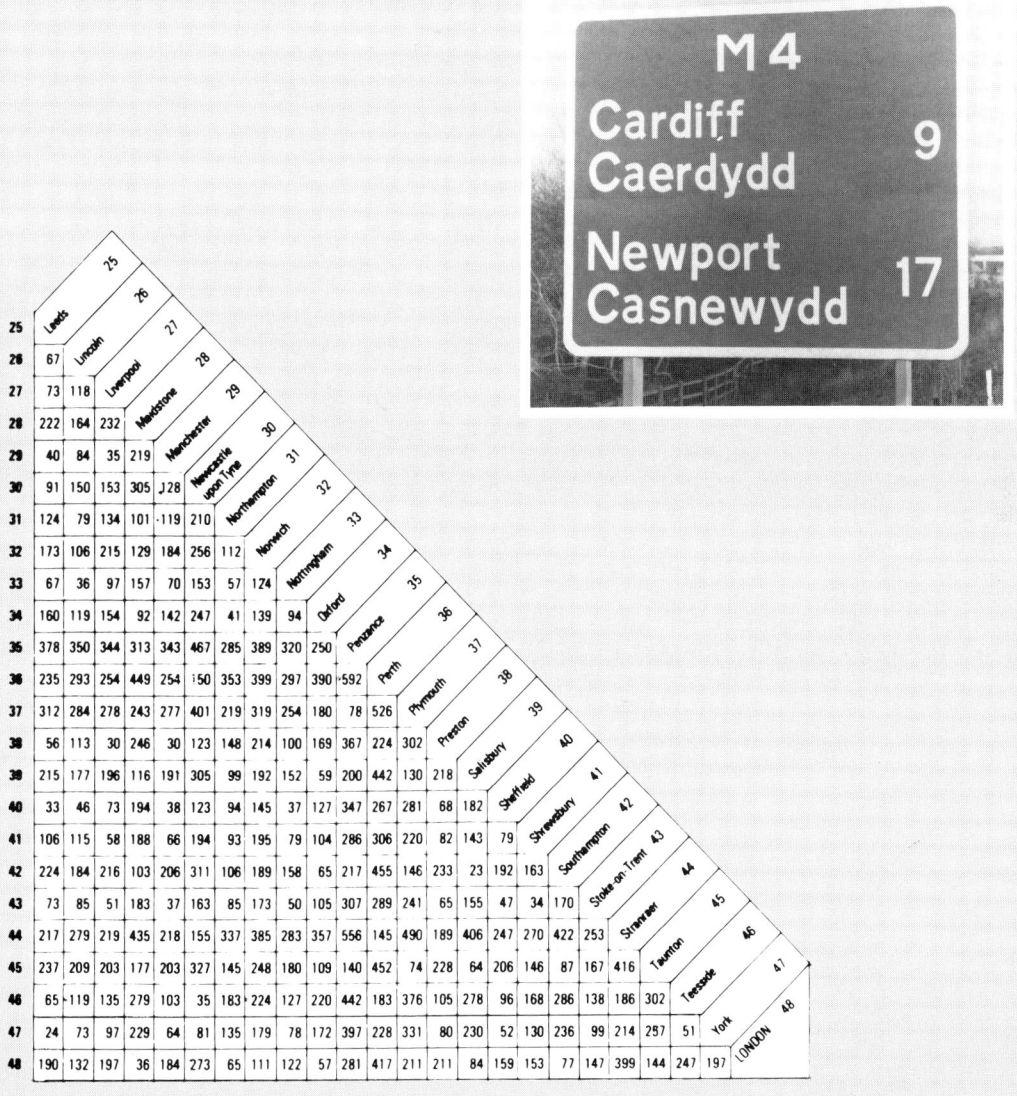

25

Swansea

Londonderry

Birmingham

Glasgow

These photographs show the second biggest cities in England, Scotland, Wales and Northern Ireland.

1 In which city are there many interesting designs for the large buildings?
2 Which two cities have a lot of space given to long-distance inland transport?
3 Why do the other two cities not need to give so much space for long-distance inland transport?
4 What recreational areas can you see in or near these four cities?
5 In what ways is Londonderry different from the other three cities?

26

BOROUGHS OF LONDON

Greater London has spread out over many old towns. These are now called *Boroughs* of London. There is the City of London (with only 5 893 people living in it) and the following 32 Boroughs:

Croydon	Outer	316 557	Newham	Inner	209 290–
Bromley	Outer	294 451	Haringey	Inner	203 175–
Barnet	Outer	292 331	Hounslow	Outer	199 782
Ealing	Outer	280 042	Harrow	Outer	195 999
Enfield	Outer	258 825	Westminster, City of	Inner	190 661–
Wandsworth	Inner	255 723–	Hackney	Inner	180 237–
Brent	Outer	251 257–	Camden	Inner	171 563–
Lambeth	Inner	245 739	Sutton	Outer	168 407
Havering	Outer	240 318	Merton	Outer	164 912
Lewisham	Inner	233 225–	Islington	Inner	159 754–
Hillingdon	Outer	229 183	Richmond upon Thames	Outer	157 867
Redbridge	Outer	225 019	Barking and Dagenham	Outer	150 175
Waltham Forest	Outer	215 092	Hammersmith and Fulham	Inner	148 054–
Bexley	Outer	214 818	Tower Hamlets	Inner	142 975–
Greenwich	Outer	211 806	Kensington and Chelsea	Inner	138 759–
Southwark	Inner	211 708–	Kingston upon Thames	Outer	132 411

1. Which London Boroughs have more people living in them than there are in Bradford?
2. How many London Boroughs have more people living in them than there are in Sunderland?
3. Which towns in Britain are about the same size as Tower Hamlets?

Discounts

Shops may offer goods at list price, or at a cut price below list price (also known as the manufacturer's recommended price or M.R.P.), or at a discount.

You may get a discount
  with a membership card of some sort,
  or from a mail order firm,
  or for spending more than a certain sum,
  or just for paying cash instead of asking for credit.
Most discounts are quoted as percentages.
If you are not sure how to work out percentages, see page 84.

HOW MUCH DO YOU SAVE ON THESE GOODS?

1. 10% discount on a new carpet M.R.P. £150.00.
2. 10% discount on a new fridge M.R.P. £120.00.
3. 10% discount on a colour television M.R.P. £280.00.
4. 10% discount on a video recorder M.R.P. £483.00.
5. 5% discount on stereo equipment worth £150.00.
6. 5% discount on a bicycle M.R.P. £120.00.
7. 5% discount on a drum set usually sold at £280.00.
8. 5% discount on a small motorcycle advertised at £483.00
9. 15% discount on a camera advertised at £150.00.
10. 15% discount on jewellery worth £280.00.

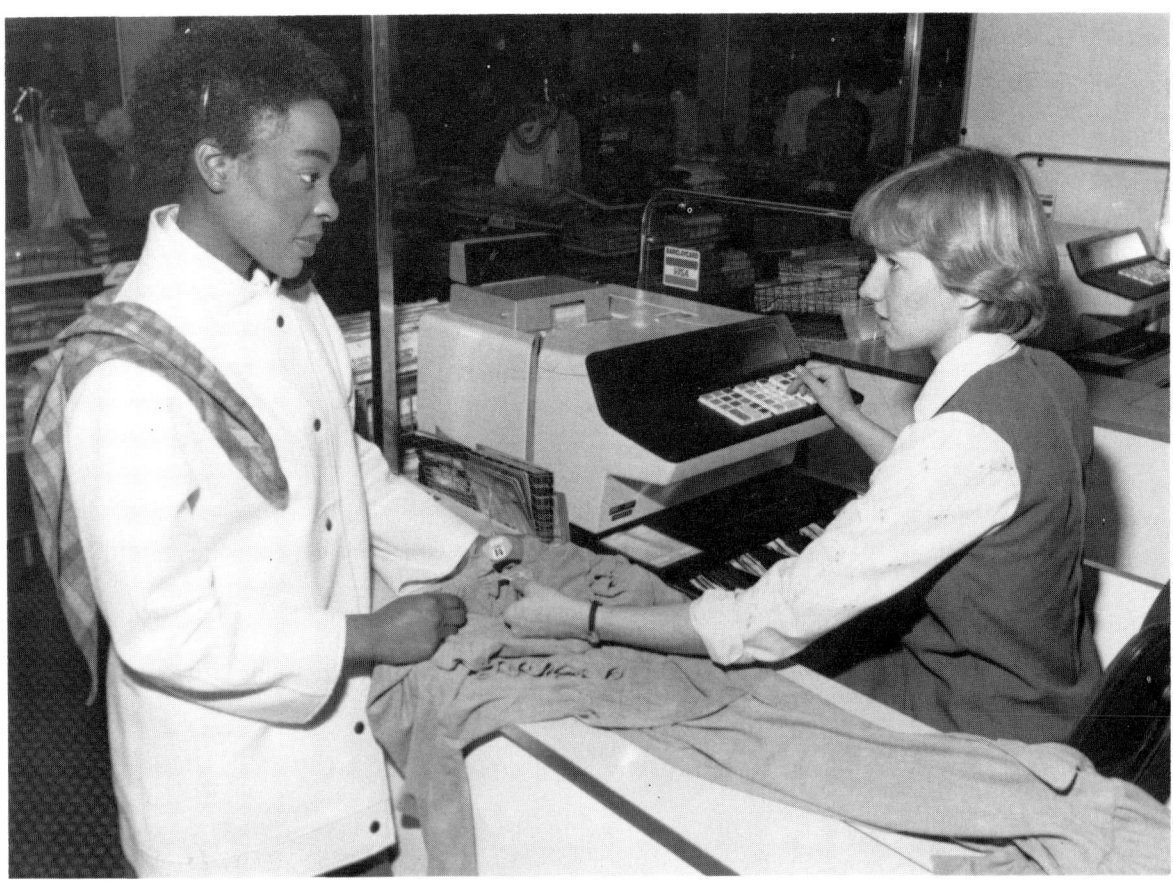

Sometimes it is cheaper to go to a shop that is selling goods at a low price; other times it is cheaper to go to a shop that will give you a cash discount on the price shown in the window.

Say you have been saving £1.00 a week for exactly a year and a half and this is all the money you have got. You can now buy a complete set of this fishing gear so long as you buy the right things at the right shops. Which shop will you go to for each item? How much will you have to pay for each item?

the fishy business CO. LTD.

CUT PRICES!

All prices include V.A.T.

LANDING NETS ONLY £8.70

Bargain TACKLE BOX £18.10

7ft Spinning rod £10.25

12½ ft float rod £25.00

KEEP NET   £9.90

✽ SPINNING REEL ✽ SPECIAL VALUE!
£7.50

Slippery Eel & Co Ltd

10% off for CASH SALES

All prices include V.A.T.

Landing nets - all yours for £9.00

Tackle box - £20.00

7ft spinning rod £12.23

12½ ft float rod £28.25

SUPER Keep net £11.50

A REAL BARGAIN!!
Spinning reel ONLY £7.50

SETTING UP HOME

These four companies all sell exactly the same brands of furniture. They are all near your home, and they all deliver free.

If you choose to buy the right things at the right shops, you can buy the items on the following list for £888.00 (remember, there are three chairs to buy, all at the same price). Which shop will you go to for each thing?

When you have answered that question, can you then suggest a way in which, by buying *more*, you can save yourself £12.50 and some trouble – you could buy a bigger load for £875.50. How?

(If you need help in planning this, the first thing to do is to work out what the lowest price is for buying each item separately, according to the discounts offered, and then to decide which shop to go to for each item and to add up the total cost).

Item	Prices advertised in			
	Homehelp P.L.C.	Cut Cost P.L.C.	MailOrder P.L.C.	Pick Your-Own P.L.C.
	Discount for orders over £1 000.00 is 15%	These are our cash prices	12% discount to agents	10% off these prices for cash
Table	£120.00	£105.00	£100.00	£110.00
Bed	£170.00	£150.00	£150.00	£160.00
3 chairs price *each*	£ 40.00	£ 40.00	£ 50.00	£ 45.00
Wardrobe	£150.00	£210.00	£220.00	£170.00
Wall unit	£230.00	£220.00	£225.00	£225.00
Settee	£200.00	£205.00	£275.00	£230.00

DISCOUNTS, V.A.T., AND DISCOUNT ON PART

While discounts are taken off, V.A.T. (Value Added Tax) has to be added on. In some deals, such as buying a new car, you may find the discount is given only on the basic price, and not on other charges and extras supplied. How much will the bills be in the end for these three customers?

	Michael	Maureen	Melanie
M.R.P of car	£3 000.00	£3 500.00	£4 100.00
discount	10%	11%	12%
delivery	£40.00	£70.00	£90.00
pre-delivery inspection	free	£50.00	£60.00
extras fitted (stainless steel exhausts &c)	£80.00	£100.00	£120.00
anti-rust treatment	£130.00	£180.00	£220.00
V.A.T.	15%	15%	15%
Road Tax (no V.A.T.)	£85.00	£85.00	£85.00
petrol (V.A.T. already included)	£10.00	£15.00	£15.00

If Michael finished with £512.50 in the bank; Maureen finished with £357.75; and Melanie only had £137.30 left, how much had each one had to begin with?

Europe, our neighbours

How many countries of Europe can you name?
How many can you find on an outline map?

1. Try a quick quiz in pairs. Don't look at the table opposite. How many of the countries on the outline map can your partner name without any help? How many can you name?
2. Trace the map below, and then fill it in like this:
   a. Look up a map of Europe (political) in an atlas.
   b. Start with country number 1. What country is it?
   c. Look at the table opposite. How may people live in that country? You will find it is less than five million.
   d. On your map, write in the name of the country; colour it in the colour you have chosen for 'less than five million'. Have other colours for 5 to 10 million, 11 to 15 million and so on.
   e. Look in the table to find what city is the capital.
   f. Write in the name of the capital by the right point on the map.
   g. Go on like this for all the other countries.
3. When you have finished your map, try the quiz again working in pairs. How much better can you score now?
4. Can you answer quiz questions about some of the things we buy from these countries.?

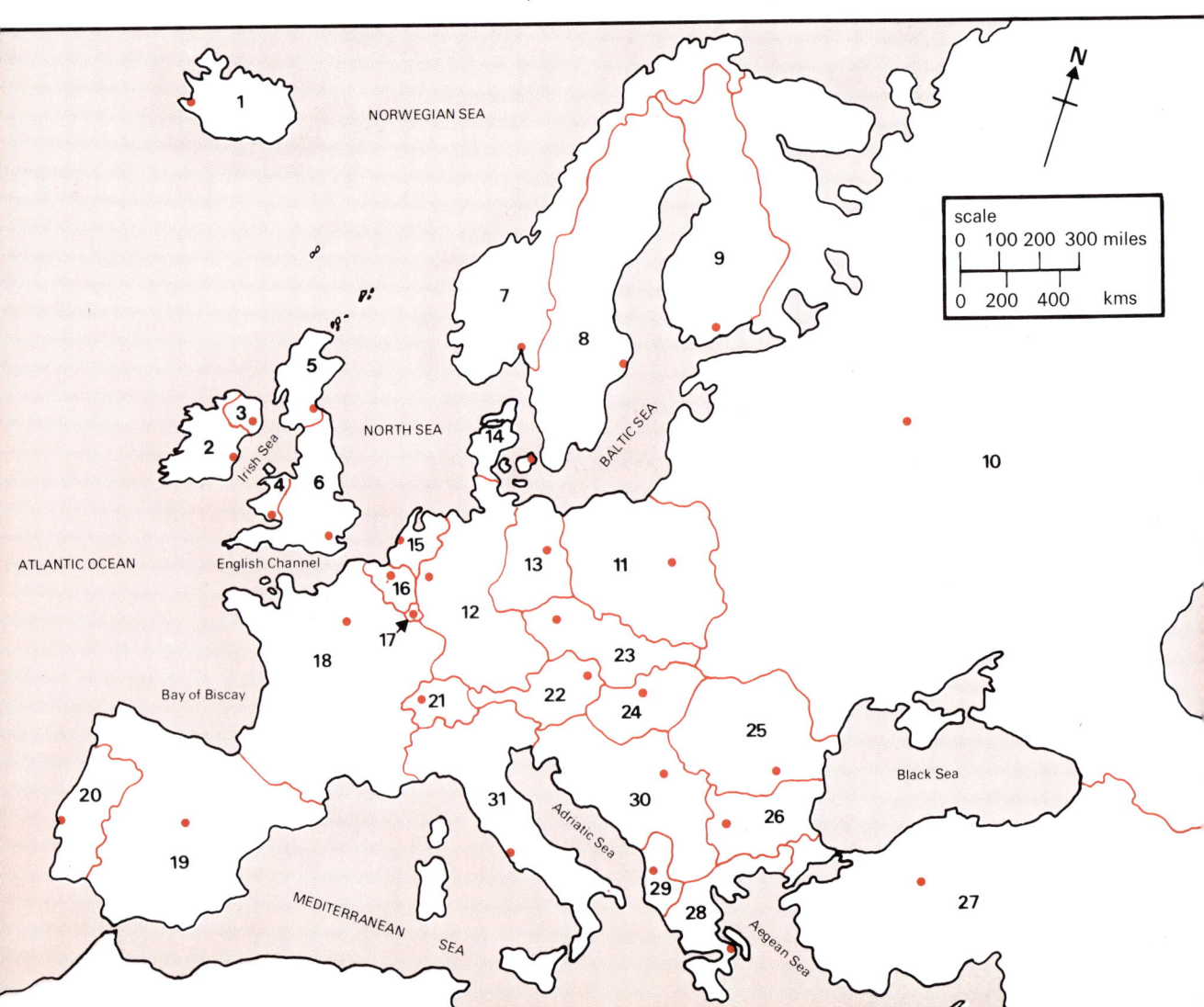

INFORMATION FOR COMPLETING THE MAP OF EUROPE WITH THE HELP OF AN ATLAS.

Country no.	Population in millions	Capital city	Part of the goods we buy from that country
1	0.2	Reykjavik	Frozen fish
2	3	Dublin	Meat, beer, textiles
3	2	Belfast	—
4	3	Cardiff	—
5	5	Edinburgh	—
6	46	London	—
7	4	Oslo	Fish, paper
8	8	Stockholm	Paper, machinery
9	5	Helsinki	Timber
10	262	Moscow	Cameras
11	35	Warsaw	Various
12	61	Bonn	Cars, machinery
13	17	East Berlin	Very little
14	5	Copenhagen	Meat
15	14	The Hague	Vegetables, electrical
16	10	Brussels	Textiles, chemicals
17	0.4	Luxembourg	Very little
18	53	Paris	Cars, machinery
19	37	Madrid	Oranges, onions
20	10	Lisbon	Wine, chestnuts
21	6	Bern	Watches, electronics
22	8	Vienna	Textiles, clothes
23	15	Prague	Very little
24	10	Budapest	Very little
25	22	Bucharest	Very little
26	9	Sofia	Very little
27	43	Ankara	Very little
28	9	Athens	Currants
29	3	Tirana	Very little
30	22	Belgrade	Very little
31	56	Rome	Cars, machinery

Find out more

1. Which countries in Europe do members of your class know about? What can they tell you about them?
   a Which ones has anyone been to?
   b Do any of you know people who have come to England from European countries?
   c Have any parents had to go abroad as part of their jobs?
2. What cars, radios, cameras, food, drink, watches, clocks or other things can you find at home or at school that have been imported from other countries in Europe? Which countries are they from?
3. Which European newspapers or magazines can you buy in your town? What countries do they come from?

Filling in forms

1
Provisional Licence
To enable you to drive motor vehicles with a view to passing a driving test. If you are a motor-cyclist you may have to take a test in two parts. You will not need a provisional licence if you hold a full licence which states that it has the effect of a provisional licence to drive other groups of vehicles.
If you are applying for your first provisional licence do not drive until you receive it.

2
Notes to help you
List for question 4b
Driving or attempting to drive while under the influence of drink or drugs.
Driving or attempting to drive with an excess of alcohol in the body.
Failure to provide a specimen of breath, blood or urine at a police station after driving or attempting to drive a motor vehicle.
Aiding or abetting one of the above offences.

3
Health
See also section on Physical and Mental Fitness in leaflet D100.
Among the reasons for answering **YES** to 6d and for giving details are:
  (i) that you have been treated for drug addiction in the last three years;
or (ii) that you have diabetes;
or (iii) that you have a heart condition or are fitted with a cardiac pacemaker.
If you have or have had epilepsy, you may still be considered for the grant of a licence if you have been free from attacks for two years (or if you have attacks while asleep you must have established a pattern of such attacks only, over a period of more than three years)

You are going to have to fill in a lot of forms in the next few years.
Try filling in some now and keep them safe so you can check them when you need them.
Make the answers as real as possible. Here are some examples. Often the small print seems to make the form hard to understand. Think about each section to see if it matters to you. If not, don't worry any more about it.

1 This is the bit you need to read. You do not need to read the note for people who have already had a full driving licence, and have lost it or want to exchange it.
Note the last sentence that says you must not start driving until the licence you are applying for has reached you.

2 Someone might have been to court for an offence, like shop-lifting. That does not have to be put down on the driving licence application. But you must put down any offence concerned with driving, including any offence concerned with driving under the influence of drugs or alcohol. Remember this must be declared for ten years: if you commit an offence now, you will have to declare it for the next ten years. 'Aiding and abetting' includes saying to a friend 'Oh, it will be all right just for once.'

3 Check your eyesight by measuring how far away you can read a number plate. To measure a distance of 67 feet or 75 feet, pace it out by putting toe to heel for each step.
Epilepsy, or petit mal, is quite common, and can be well controlled by tablets. You must say if you have been having treatment.
'Your estate in the hands of a receiver . . .' means that you have been made bankrupt and are not allowed to carry on your own business affairs.

Application for a Driving Licence

Department of Transport

Please do not write above this line

D1 Oct/82

Please read Notes then complete in **BLACK INK** and **BLOCK LETTERS**

Notes to help you

If you need more information before you fill in this form please ask at your post office for leaflet D100

To drive a heavy goods vehicle or a public service vehicle you need an additional licence. Consult a Traffic Area Office.

1 Applicant

a. Surname: **BEATON**
   Christian or forenames: **DAN GERALD**

   Please tick box or state other title such as Dr, Rev.

b. Mr ✓ 1   Mrs ☐ 2   Miss ☐ 3
   Other title: _____

   Your full permanent address in Great Britain (see note on left)

c. Address: **45 UNFINISHED ROAD**
   MARSKE-BY-THE-SEA
   Post Town: **CLEVELAND**
   Postcode (Your licence may be delayed if the postcode is not quoted): **TS11 8Q7**

d. Please tick box: Male ✓ 1   Female ☐ 2

e. Please enter your date of birth: Day **25** Month **09** Year **66**

f. Have you ever held a British licence (full or provisional)? Answer either YES or NO: **NO**

   If YES, please enter your Driver Number (if known) in the box below (and make a separate note of it).

2 Licence required

a. Please tick the type of licence you require (see note 'Types of licence' on left)
   Full ☐   Provisional ✓   Duplicate ☐   Exchange ☐

b. Please tick box if you also require provisional motorcycle entitlement (see IMPORTANT note on left). ✓

c. When do you want your new licence to begin? A licence cannot be backdated. Application may be made during the 2 months before commencement date.
   Day **25** Month **09** Year **83**

d. If you have passed a driving test since the issue of your last licence write the new Group passed here _____ and enclose the pass certificate.

3 Last Licence

Please give details of your last GB licence and enclose it, or any EEC licence, with this form.

a. If your last licence was surrendered on disqualification write S/D or if you have not previously held a licence, write NONE _____

b. Type of licence i.e. Provisional or Full _____

c. Expiry date _____

d. If your last licence has been lost, stolen, destroyed or defaced please tick the appropriate box below. If a lost licence is later found and is still current you must return it to DVLC but keep any licence issued to you in the meantime.

   Lost or Stolen ☐   Destroyed ☐   Defaced and I enclose it ☐

e. Name and/or address on licence if different from that at 1 above
   Surname: _____
   Christian or forenames: _____
   Address: _____
   Post Town: _____
   Postcode (please quote): _____

Official Use Only

Provisional-1 Full-2   Rec. type
Cont. No.
MC
DRE   End
Iss. No.
TPC
Ent.
MP   RE   VDOB
MIM   Amount
DAM

Notes to help you

1 Applicant
Surname: your last name
forenames: all your other names
postcode: if you do not know it, ask at the Post Office.
month: January = 01
February = 02
March = 03
April = 04
May = 05
June = 06
July = 07
August = 08
September = 09
October = 10
November = 11
December = 12

2 Types of licence
If this is the first time you have applied for a licence, tick the box. If you had one before but failed the test, leave it blank.
You are not allowed to apply for a licence more than two months before you need it, and you cannot have a provisional licence until your seventeenth birthday.

3 Lost licence
If you did have a licence before you must fill in this section

Please continue overleaf

4 Disqualifications and endorsements
See the note on page 34. Dan Beaton had a clear record. You must enter the details if your record is not clear.

5 Health
See the note on page 34. Many people have disabilities, which may not stop them driving safely. You should mention anything that you think would come under this heading.

6 Declaration
You will be fined if you put down anything that you know is not true on this form.

Failure to answer ALL the questions on this page may result in delay

4 Disqualifications and Endorsements

a. Are you disqualified by a Court from holding or obtaining a driving licence?

Answer either YES or NO [**NO**]   If YES, give date and period of disqualification _____

Court _____

b. Has a Court ordered you to be disqualified or your licence to be endorsed for **ANY** offence in the last **4** years (or in the last **11** years for any offence in the list on the left)?

Answer either YES or NO [**NO**]   If YES give details of all disqualifications and endorsements

Date of conviction _____ Court _____
Offence _____
Date of conviction _____ Court _____
Offence _____

If necessary state other disqualifications/endorsements (or details of successful appeals) on a separate sheet; da sign it and enclose it with this application.

If you enclose a separate sheet please tick box [ ]

5 Eyesight

Can you read a vehicle number plate in good daylight (with glasses if worn), at 75 feet for figures 3½" high or a feet for figures 3¼" high?

Answer either YES or NO [**YES**]   (If **NO** you may still be able to obtain a licence for a pedestrian contr vehicle or a mowing machine—see leaflet D100)

6 Health   Questions 6a - 6d **MUST** be answered

a. Have you ever had a licence refused or revoked for medical reasons?

Answer either YES or NO [**NO**]   If YES give date and reasons _____

If you are in doubt about your answers to 6b, 6c or 6d consult your doctor

b. Has a doctor ever advised you not to drive?

Answer either YES or NO [**NO**]   If YES give details _____

c. Are you without hand or foot or have you any defect in limb movement or power?

Answer either YES or NO [   ]   If YES give details _____

If the answer is **YES** and you have held a licence before,
(i) was this limb disability mentioned in your previous application? Answer either YES or NO _____
(ii) If so, has it got worse since then? Answer either YES or NO _____

d. Have you now or have you ever had
(i) epilepsy or sudden attacks of disabling giddiness or fainting or any mental illness or defect

Answer either YES or NO [**NO**]

(ii) or any other disability or medical condition which could affect your fitness as a driver either now or in the fu (see note 'Health' on left)

Answer either YES or NO [**NO**]

If the answer to either question is **YES** give details _____

7 Declaration

WARNING. You are liable to prosecution if you knowingly make a false statemen obtain a driving licence or do not give details of current endorsements. So is any else who knowingly makes a false statement to help you obtain one.

I apply for a driving licence.

I enclose the fee of £ _____ (if applicable. See notes on left)   Postal Order/Cheque no _____

I declare that I have checked the answers given in this application, that to the best of my knowledge and belie correct, and that I am not disqualified by reason of age or otherwise from holding or obtaining the licence for w applying.

Signature of Applicant _____*D.G. Beaton*_____   Date __1.8.83__

- If you are enclosing an EEC licence which entitles you to drive heavy goods (HGV) or Public Servic vehicles and you wish to drive any such vehicles in Great Britain you will need a GB HGV or PSV l Please tick this box [ ] and make a separate application to the Traffic Area Office in which area reside as soon as possible.

If this is your **FIRST** application for a British driving licence, please send this for First Application Section, DVLC, SWANSEA, SA99 1AD.
OTHERWISE, send it to: Driver Licence Section, DVLC, SWANSEA, SA99 1AB.

APPLICATION FOR BRITISH VISITOR'S PASSPORT

You need a passport to go to any foreign country except the Republic of Ireland (Eire). No passport at all is needed for some day trips to France and Belgium. You can choose between having a British Visitor's Passport, which is cheaper but only lasts for one year, and having a United Kingdom Passport, which costs more but lasts for ten years. Try to look at a copy of a complete form so that you can read all the explanatory notes.

Make tracings of the spaces on the application form shown here, and fill in what would be the right answers for:

a Diane Mary Williams, of 19 Deermoss Road, Aberystwyth, Dyfed, SY23 1WZ. She is single, and was born on 19 May 1964 at Port Talbot. She is 5 feet 3 inches (1.60 metres) tall, and has auburn hair and a small scar on her left cheek. She has not had a passport before, but now wants one to travel to France, Belgium and Holland.

Notes to help you

Section 1
Surname: Your last name.
Forenames: All your other names.
Postcode: If you do not know it, ask at the Post Office.
Height: Measure it without your shoes on.
Visible distinguishing marks: Colour of eyes, permanent scars, or moles or other marks that are always there.
Town of birth: Do you know which it was? Can you spell it?

Section 3
Children, relationship to applicant: Usually parents will put down their sons or daughters, but these may be step-sons or step-daughters, or on occasion someone might include nephew, niece, or cousin.

Section 5
If a child between the age of 8 and 16 is to have his or her own passport, he or she must sign this section at the office where the passport will be given out.

37

Section 6
Where there are two lines of small print, choose the words that fit what you want, and cross out the other words.

Section 7
You only fill this section in if you have lost another passport.

Section 8
You must tick the countries that you want to visit. You can visit as many of these countries as you like. If you want to visit any other country you will have to have an ordinary British passport, which will cost you more, and is applied for on a different form.

---

6 DECLARATION (Read carefully – make **no** alterations other than any appropriate deletions at * and §).

A I the undersigned, hereby apply for the issue of a British Visitor's Passport to myself*/the child* named in section 1 and declare that the information given in this application is correct to the best of my knowledge and belief

B I am*/the child is* a British subject and citizen of the United Kingdom and Colonies, § as is my wife*/husband* ⎫

C No other application is being made for a passport for myself*/the child*, no valid passport is held by me*/the child*, nor   ⎬ see note (x) on Page 4.
is a passport of mine*/the child* held by any official. ⎭

D No outstanding debt to Her Majesty's Government in respect of any repatriation, or like relief, has been incurred on behalf of any person named in this application.

E I have read and understood the Notes on pages 3 and 4.

F I have ticked in Section 8 all the countries intended to be visited on this British Visitor's Passport

WARNING—Applicants for British Visitor's Passports are warned that it is a criminal offence for any person to make a statement which is to his knowledge untrue for the purpose of procuring a passport

NOTE: A child under 16 is not the applicant (see Note (v)(f)) .... Signature of applicant ....

Date .... § Signature of wife/husband ....

*Delete as appropriate   § Delete references in italics to wife/husband if she/he is not to be included in the Passport

7 PARTICULARS OF PREVIOUS PASSPORT OR BRITISH VISITOR'S PASSPORT WHICH IS STILL VALID BUT WHICH HAS BEEN LOST, MISLAID OR IS NOT AVAILABLE:

* Passport No. .... issued at .... on ....
* British Visitor's Passport No. ....

Bearer's names at time of issue ....

Circumstances in which passport was lost, mislaid or destroyed, or other reason for its non-availability
....

Place and date of loss ....

Has loss been reported to the Police? .... If so, state where and when ....

I certify that the above particulars are correct and undertake in the event of the passport coming again into my possession to return it immediately to the Passport Office, London, to a British Consulate or to a British High Commissioner's Office for cancellation.

Signature .... Date ....

* Delete as appropriate

8 COUNTRIES FOR WHICH BRITISH VISITOR'S PASSPORTS ARE VALID—TICK BOX OF EACH COUNTRY TO BE VISITED OR TRAVELLED THROUGH.

☐ ANDORRA	☐ DENMARK (including Faroe Islands and Greenland)
☐ AUSTRIA	☐ FINLAND
☐ BELGIUM	☐ ICELAND — Visits by holders of British Visitor's Passports to this
☐ FRANCE (including Corsica)	☐ NORWAY group of countries as a whole must not exceed three
☐ GIBRALTAR	☐ SWEDEN months in any nine-month period.
☐ ITALY (including Sicily, Sardinia and Elba)	☐ GREECE (including the Greek Islands) — A British Visitor's Passport is valid for Greece and Turkey but travellers proceeding overland through
☐ LIECHTENSTEIN	☐ TURKEY countries bordering Greece and Turkey should have an ordinary British passport.
☐ LUXEMBOURG	
☐ MALTA	☐ FEDERAL REPUBLIC OF GERMANY (WEST GERMANY) (and for travellers by air only, the Western Sectors of Berlin). — Travellers to the German Democratic Republic (East Germany) or East Berlin, or proceeding by rail or road between the Federal Republic of Germany (West Germany) and West Berlin, must have an ordinary British passport.
☐ MONACO	
☐ NETHERLANDS	
☐ PORTUGAL (including Madeira and the Azores)	
☐ SAN MARINO	☐ BERMUDA — An ordinary British passport should be held for any visits to the United States of America.
☐ SPAIN (including the Balearic and the Canary Islands)	☐ CANADA — Travellers to Canada should note additionally that their British Visitor's Passport must be valid for one month beyond the last date they will be in Canada.
☐ SWITZERLAND	

Holders of British Visitor's Passports may travel to or from any of the above countries via the REPUBLIC OF IRELAND

IMPORTANT—IF TRAVEL TO OR THROUGH A COUNTRY NOT LISTED ABOVE IS INTENDED, APPLICATION MUST BE MADE FOR AN ORDINARY PASSPORT (FEE £11)

Now fill in application forms for the following:

b Thomas Gino Odufesco, of 108 Long Acres, Barnsley, South Yorkshire, S70 3SD. He is single, and was born on 17 November 1964 at St Helens. He is 5 feet 10 inches tall (1.78 metres), and has a mole on his forehead. He wants the passport so that he can visit France, Italy and Germany. His previous passport is no longer valid.

c Yourself. If you are not really planning to go abroad just yet, pretend you are going to Corsica.

HOLIDAY FORMS

Holiday forms often have a lot of boxes to tick or fill in. To practise on this one, pretend you are going with three friends and two dogs, driving a 1980 Morris Ital 1.3 L, overall length 14 ft 3 in, overall height 4 ft 7¾ ins, overall width 5 ft 4½ ins, registration number HQP 849W, full market value £3800. You would like to book on the London to Inverness service, leaving London on a Tuesday at 2105 hrs and reaching Inverness on Wednesday at 0916 hrs. The return train leaves Inverness at 1820 hrs on Wednesday to reach London at 0524 hrs on Thursday. Second class, two-berth sleepers cost £198.00 return for car and driver, £52.00 return for each adult, and £16.00 return for each child.

MOTORAIL BOOKING FORM — Private Cars & Motor Caravans Ø

FOR OFFICE USE — forward / return

BLOCK CAPITALS PLEASE

Mr/Ms* Initials
Address
(Business)
Telephone No. (Home)

Travel details — from / time / day/date / to
Forward journey
Alternative
Return journey
Alternative
*1st class/2nd class   *Smoking/Non-smoking   age of child under 16   Sleeper # berths required

Driver and passenger names
Mr/Ms* (surname and initials)
Driver — Yes/No*
Passenger — Yes/No*
Passenger — Yes/No*
Passenger — Yes/No*
Passenger — Yes/No*
Passenger

other tickets required _____ dog(s) please state number travelling

On behalf of all persons named above, I, being 18 years of age or more, accept the Booking conditions and enclose:
*(a) my party's full remittance for   £
OR *(b) deposit of £20 (balance to be paid not later than 28 days before date of travel)   £
AND *(c) Package Travel Insurance at £4.15, £4.70 or £5.25 per person   £
*(d) Motor Vehicle in Transit Insurance premiums (see page 29)   £
Total £

Railcard: Type _____ No. _____
I wish to pay by credit card †
Please charge my ACCESS/ BARCLAYCARD/ AMERICAN EXPRESS Account No.

Date
Signature
Cheques, postal or money orders should be crossed and made payable to 'British Rail' or to your booking agent.

Car details
registration number
make
model   year 19
overall length (including tow bar if fitted)   ft   in
overall width   ft   in
overall height (including roof rack if fitted)   ft   in
full market value of car £
Luggage Trailer/ Boat on Trailer (dimensions)   ft   in

Metric Equivalents
Maximum heights for cars are shown in metres. The feet-and-inches equivalents are:
2.15m — 7ft 0in.
1.98m — 6ft 6in.
1.63m — 5ft 4in.

Notes:
Ø Separate application form to be used for Small Commercial Vans and Trade Cars.
* Delete as necessary.
† Not applicable to bookings effected on clients' behalf by travel agents.
# Child under 5 years occupying separate sleeping berth is charged child's fare.

39

BENEFIT FORMS

If you are unable to find work, or if your work is very badly paid, and you are therefore short of money, there are a number of different sorts of benefit you can apply for. These benefits are paid by the Government from taxes.

If you want to claim benefit, the people who work in the Department of Health and Social Security will want to know what money you have got, and what expenses you have to meet. School leavers will need to complete form B1, and older people complete form SB1. These forms ask for name and address and National Insurance number. When you have filled this in, you will have an interview with one of the staff from the Department of Health and Social Security. It is a good idea to take to this interview any bank and savings books you may have, and receipts for money spent on rent, heating, and other essential expenses.

There are a number of other benefits that some young people may claim. A complete list of benefits is shown in the booklet NP 12, which is called *School leavers and students: What you pay and what you get.*

There are some benefits that your parents can claim if you stay on at school beyond the school leaving age. These include fares to school if you live more than three miles away, free dental treatment and glasses. If your parents are said to be hard up on a 'means test' (which works out their income and their expenses) you may, in some parts of the country, be able to claim an allowance, free school meals and some money towards clothing.

Other benefits you may be able to claim if they concern you include supplementary benefit, rent rebates, maternity grants and a maternity allowance, child benefit and family income supplement.

What benefits might be paid to the following people?

1. Ranjit is sixteen, and has just left school but cannot find any work.
2. Prue is seventeen, out of work and expecting a baby.
3. Norma's parents have moved away and now she has to pay the rent on the flat. She is only paid £30.00 a week for a part time job, and she is suffering from toothache.
4. Hannah is staying on at school. Her father is unemployed and her mother earns £35.00 a week in a part time job. She has two younger brothers who are also at school. Hannah lives four miles from her school.
5. Damian is staying on at school beyond school leaving age and his parents are not particularly hard up, but it has been discovered that he will be needing glasses.

NP 12/Sept 80

Social security
School leavers and students
What you pay and what you get

SB 1/Nov 81

Cash Help
how to claim supplementary benefit

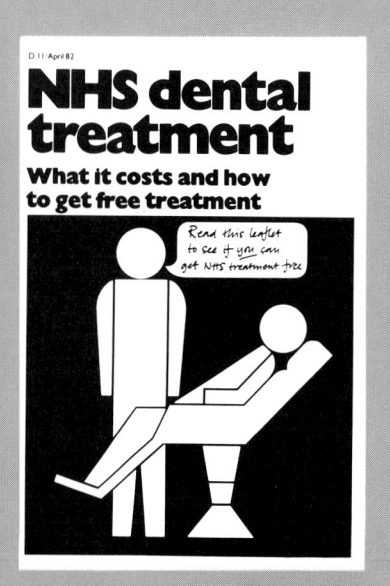

G 11/April 82
NHS glasses
How much they cost and how to get them free

NI 17A/Mar 82
Maternity grant and maternity allowance

D 11/April 82
NHS dental treatment
What it costs and how to get free treatment

41

Filling in an income tax form

The tax form is sent to everyone who has a National Insurance card. It is sent by the local tax office. The office is a branch of the Inland Revenue, which is run by the Government.

The Government pays for many things we all need, like roads and the health services. It pays for the defence of the country, runs the nationalised industries like electricity supply and the Post Office, and, with local government, helps to run many other services like schools. The money to pay for all this is raised by taxes as well as charges to customers.

Most people at work have some of their pay taken away each week or each month (PAYE = Pay As You Earn). This saves them facing a big tax bill at the end of the year.

We all benefit from the services the Government provides and so we all pay a share of the cost. If people are unhappy about the taxes they pay, they can vote for a new Government in an election (see page 124). A new Government can provide more, or fewer, services or share out the cost in different ways.

The tax form worries a lot of people.
Filling it in may take a little while.
But it is usually quite easy for people who have ordinary jobs, or those who are not lucky enough to get a job. Just remember to keep all the important papers about money during the year. Have a file for them, and put in the file all the papers like payslips, bank statements, and statements of interest on your account.

The form has a number of sections where you have to write down everything you have earned or profits you have made during the year. It also has a number of sections where you claim "expenses" and "allowances" which are ways in which you are let off paying quite so much tax.

The tax inspector's job is to make sure everyone pays a fair share. The Government decides what a fair share is. Many elections are fought about taxes. It is your chance to have a say about who should pay what.

The tax form has numbers beside each section. You can follow the same numbers on the "Tax Return Guide" to find out what the rules are for each section. You can keep a copy of your return by filling in the columns on the Tax Return Guide. Most of the rules on the Guide will only make a difference for people with complicated business deals.

The form you have to fill in will be for a year that ends at the beginning of April. (This is called a financial year). If you have an ordinary job you will have paid tax already during the year on PAYE (Pay As You Earn). Your employer has to take this off your pay. Filling in the form allows the tax inspector to check that you have paid the right amount. You may get some tax paid back, while some other people may have to pay a little more. If you do not fill in an income tax form you will pay tax on all your earnings apart from the single person's allowance.

At the end of the financial year your employer will give you a special payslip called a P60. You must keep this carefully because it gives the total figures that the tax office needs.

The tax return is always dated for the year you are in, but the information wanted is for the last year. On the form dated 1983–4, for example, the tax inspector wants information about what happened during 1982–3, and so on.

TRY FILLING IN A FORM

Practise filling in a form. Put in as much real information as you can. When you have not got real information to use, put in the figures for Sam Pound.

Use your own name and address. If you do not know your post-code, ask at the Post Office. Your "works no., if any" will be shown on your pay-slip.

Sam Pound's employer is HANDIMAKE P.L.C.
Sam's job is Apprentice Engineer, and his works no. is 47–156.
Susan Dollar's employer is SELLWELL P.L.C.
Her job is Sales Manager, and her works no. is 32–145.

Earnings
Employers have to tell the Inland Revenue what your total pay for the past year was. Sam's was £4 375.64, but he doesn't need to put this on the form. He is not married. Susan's total pay was £4 410.80. There are no other earnings – Sam isn't lucky enough to get tips in the factory. If Sam had a Saturday job or earned money in the evenings the amount would have to be included here. Other perks, like luncheon vouchers, have to be put in here.

Expenses
Sam's Union has agreed a fixed sum (£20.00 p.a.) for working clothes, so put an X in the 'self' box. Susan has nothing to claim here. Everyone wants to be able to claim other expenses, but few are allowed unless you are running your own business. You cannot claim the cost of going to work.

Fees and subscriptions
Sam buys a paper called *Apprentice Engineer* (£1.00 a week) and a magazine called *Design Expert* (£2.00 quarterly) because he needs to read them for his work at the College. (How much do the papers cost in a year?) He is also a Member of the Institute of Factory Engineers, which costs him £18.00 a year. He has receipts for all these expenses.

Pensions
Usually only for old folk.

Social Security Pensions and benefits
Unemployment and supplementary benefits received must be included so that if they bring your income for the year up to a high enough figure, tax will be charged. You do not need to include child benefit, sickness benefit or family income supplement.

Interest
Many young people are like Sam and Susan and have an account at the Post Office with the National Savings Bank. You must write down how much interest has been paid (and you may have to send your book up to find out – you can do this from the Post Office). In fact no tax is likely to be paid unless you have had more than £1 250.00 in the account for a whole year. Many other people have money in a Building Society and have been told that they will not pay tax on the interest. This is true (until your pay reaches £300.00 a week), but even so the tax inspector wants to know how much has been paid. Fill it in, although it won't be counted as part of your income. If you receive interest from money in other accounts, you must fill in the details. This may be taxable, so you may be sent a bill for the tax due.

Sam has an ordinary National Savings Bank account. He usually has about £80.00 in it, so he only got £4.10 interest for the year. He has his savings in the Sinking Sands Building Society, and they paid him £54.25 interest. He has no other accounts. Susan has a bit more in her National Savings account and got £7.13 interest. She does not have a Building Society account, but she got £83.20 interest on an account with Money Grabber Trust and Savings P.L.C. which she must declare and pay tax on.

Dividends
Anyone can buy shares in a public company, and then they get a share in the profit the company makes (if it makes any). This is called a dividend, and you must put it down and pay tax on it. Sam and Susan both cross this section out, with nothing to declare.

Rents, Profits, Payments, Other Income
These are all sections that Sam and Susan can cross out, but they should put a separate line for each numbered item. A friend of their's who is setting up her own business will have a lot to put in here.

Outgoings
Interest on loans. The only interest you can usually set against tax is the interest you pay on a mortgage, and the bank or building society who gave you the mortgage will tell the Inland Revenue how much that was. Sam lives in a rented flat and cannot claim that. Susan has a mortgage and paid £825.00 interest last year.

Maintenance
This section deals with money paid out when married couples are separated or divorced. It does not affect Sam and Susan.

Deed of Covenant
If you give some money to a charity on Deed of Covenant, the Inland Revenue pays the charity the tax you have already paid on that money (if you pay tax at the standard rate). You don't get tax back, but the charity does. Fill in this section for the tax inspector's information. Sam has a Covenant to give £10.00 a year to the Red Cross and Susan has one to give £15.00 a year to Age Concern.

Capital gains
Not a section to concern Sam and Susan, but an important one for people buying and selling things worth more than £3 000.00 (apart from their own homes and private cars).

Allowances
The only allowance that Sam and Susan can claim is the single person's allowance. If they get married they will claim the married man's allowance instead.

If you have now filled in their tax forms for them, you should be able to work out how much tax they should have paid during the year. The way to do this is to lay out the figures like this:

Taxable income (the interest from the National Savings Bank and Building Society was not taxed) ... ... £_____

Less

Expenses ... ... £_____

Single person's allowance ... ... £1 565.00 for that year

Total ... ... £_____

Take this away from taxable income ... ... £_____

Remainder is the amount on which tax is due ... ... £_____

The tax rate that year was 30%, so work out 30% of this amount

= £_____

which is the amount of tax which should have been paid.

In fact Sam had paid £875.78 on PAYE and Susan had paid £714.20. Will they be glad or sorry to hear from the tax inspector? How big is the difference for each of them?

Finding out by phone

There are many useful things that you can find out on the phone. It is quicker and cheaper than going to see for yourself. If you get a chance to practise some of these, here's how. You will need the small telephone book of the S.T.D. codes for your area, as well as your local telephone directory. (See page 14 of this book for more details). Find out what numbers are needed to fill the gaps here.

> Hey! The clock's stopped! Isn't it later than that?

> Let's phone up the speaking clock.

> What number? The little book of course!

> Here it is: ___ Dial away then.

> At the third stroke it will be three twenty two and ten seconds. pip! pip! pip! At the third stroke it will be...

> GOSH! Fancy going on like that all day.

Directory enquiries 192
cheap rate from 6pm
Dialling code Paris 010331
Speaking clock ___

A DAY OUT? THE MONEY DOESN'T MATTER!

Scene: A bit after 8.00 a.m. at Weston super Mare on a Saturday morning in February.

Sam: Hey! The clock's stopped. Isn't it later than that?

Lin: Let's phone up the speaking clock.

Sam: What number? – The little book, of course.

Lin: Here it is. Dial _____.

Phone: At the third stroke it will be eight twenty nine and thirty seconds.

Sam: Gosh! Fancy going on like that all day. That gives us half an hour to get on our way. Is it going to rain?

Lin: Where? Here, on the way, or in London?

Sam: All of them really.

Lin: Well, get phoning again. You'll want the areas for Bristol and London I suppose. Dial _____ first and then _____ _____.

Sam: Snow! I'd not expected that. Snow all the way. Do you think the road's blocked?

Lin: My turn to phone. I'll phone Motoring Information.

Sam: That'll be _____ for the Bristol area and _____ _____ for London.

Lin: Blocked! Everything snowed up. So we can't go! What shall we do?

Sam: Train! Phone British Rail. That's _____.

Lin: Stopped! Snow has stopped them all.

Sam: Let's go skiing! Take a plane to Scotland. Come on!

Lin: Yes, but is the snow any good for skiing in Scotland?

Sam: Let's find out. Let's dial _____ _____.

Lin: What did I tell you! It's raining in the Cairngorms. Warmer there than it is here. That's no go.

Sam: Bother! Well, I'm going to do some cooking. What shall I make?

Lin: Don't know. Let's dial for a recipe. That's _____.

Sam: Oh no! It says I should be digging a trench for my runner beans. Why isn't it telling me what to cook?

Lin: Because you didn't read the code book carefully. When is that number used for recipes and when is it used for gardening?

Can you tell me if the trains to London are running?

Sorry, luv, the line's blocked. Nothing is getting through.

Thank you.

47

LONG-DISTANCE SHOPPING

When you phone to a place where a lot of people work, you must make it clear who you want to speak to. You must expect to be put through from one person to another at the other end, and there is no point in making your main request until you are speaking to the right person.

Try to get your tone of voice right and your speech clear in this practice conversation.

Directory Enquiries. Which town? — I'd like a number in Oxford please.

What name? — The shop, Ellistons.

What address? — Cornmarket.

It's 43161. — Thank you, goodbye. What's the code for Oxford, then? Ah yes. It's 0865. And the number was 43161. So I dial 0865 43161.

Ellistons. Can I help you? — Can you give me the furniture department please?

It's ringing for you — Thank you.

Furniture department. — I hear you have got some super bedroom furniture, and as I'm coming to Oxford tomorrow I'd like to know what you have got in stock.

Yes, Madam, we have some very high quality real mahogany complete suites for only £1 499. I can really recommend them. — Oh good, I must come and see them. That sounds just what I wanted. Thank you so much. Goodbye.

1 Make your own conversation along these lines for
   a a couple phoning a store to see if wardrobes are cheaper there than elsewhere and if they can buy them on H.P.
   b a man phoning at 11.00 a.m. after he has taken the morning off work to wait for a workman who was due to come at 8.30 a.m. He wants to know if he has got to wait at home any longer.
   c a woman phoning a builder's merchant from her home to order five cubic metres of crushed stone for the drive.

2 There are six signals you may hear when you are phoning. Match the right description to the meaning of the signal.
   Meanings: (a) ringing (b) engaged (c) unobtainable (d) ringing in another country (e) ready to dial (f) time to pay (in a call box).
   Descriptions: a continuous purring; a repeated burr-burr; a steady note without a break; rapid pips; a loud single note repeated at short intervals; a loud single note with two-second intervals.

3 What do receptionists mean when they say (a) It's ringing for you (b) Will you hold? (c) Can we call you back?

Gardening

THE TOOLS FOR THE JOB

Here are some of the most useful tools for the job, with the prices that were often charged in 1982. Use the information you have been given to make a list of them with drawings, showing what they are used for, like this:

No.	Name	Price now	Job it is for

Names secateurs, rake, shovel, trowel, long arm, hoe, dutch-hoe, spade, shears, fork.

Prices (1982) No. 1 £10.98 No. 2 £12.50 No. 3 £4.00 No. 4 £6.99 No. 5 £1.50 No. 6 £8.90 No. 7 £8.95 No. 8 £7.45 No. 9 £8.90 No. 10 £6.95

Jobs pushing through weeds; pulling through weeds; digging clods; digging and breaking; powdering soil; moving piles of earth; cutting back bushes; cutting back taller trees; trimming edges and hedges; moving plants.

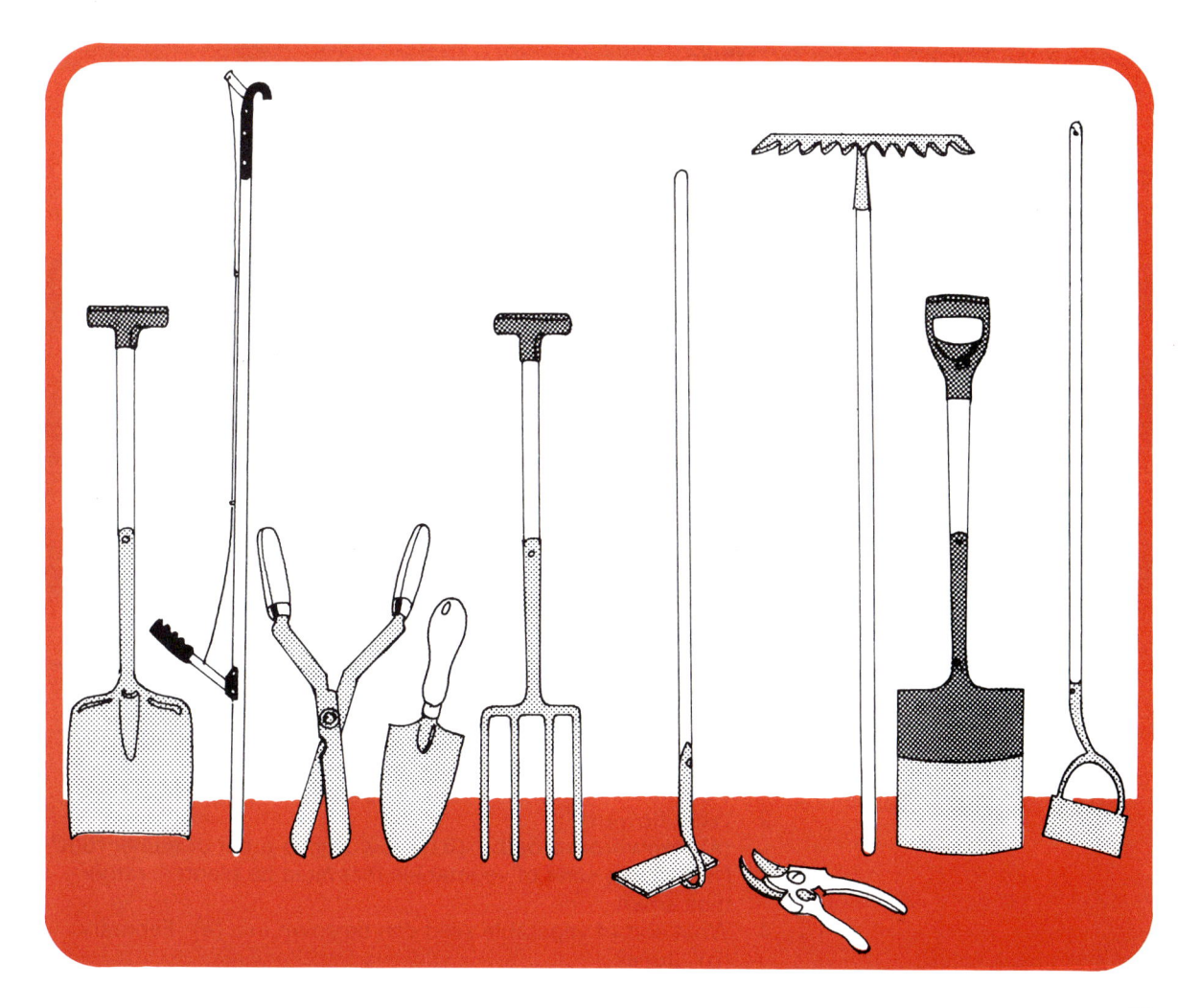

PLANTS TO RECOGNISE

It's important to be able to recognise common garden plants. It's important too to be able to recognise the common weeds. Look up any in this list that you do not know. You will find pictures of them in gardening books, magazines, and catalogues, and the weeds will be shown in books of wild flowers. Some of them are shown here – which are they?

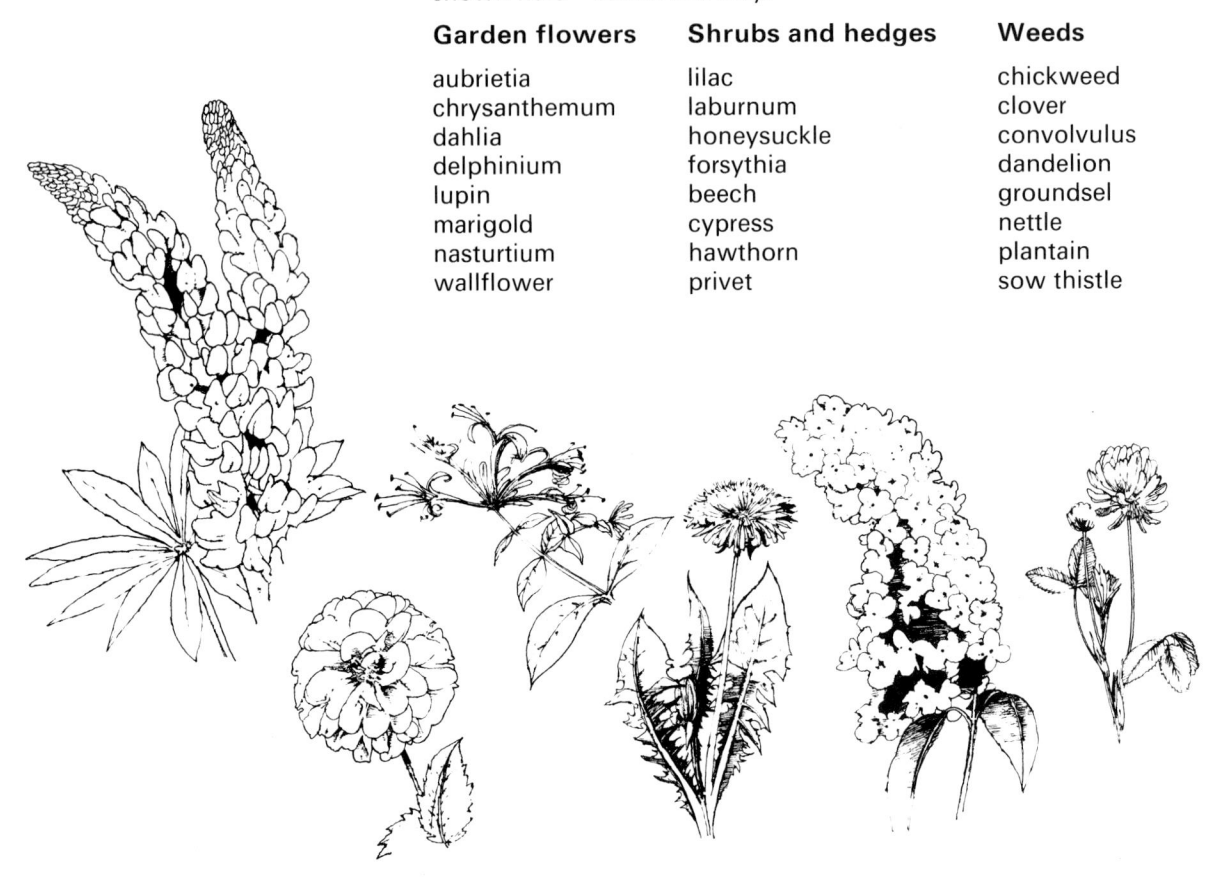

Garden flowers	Shrubs and hedges	Weeds
aubrietia	lilac	chickweed
chrysanthemum	laburnum	clover
dahlia	honeysuckle	convolvulus
delphinium	forsythia	dandelion
lupin	beech	groundsel
marigold	cypress	nettle
nasturtium	hawthorn	plantain
wallflower	privet	sow thistle

KEEP A GARDEN TIDY

Is there a garden you can help keep tidy? Your own? At school? A pensioner's? If so, look up how to do these jobs in one of the gardening books in the library:
(a) sowing seeds (b) transplanting young plants (c) weeding the borders (d) pruning the bushes

Find out from the books the answers to these questions:
1. What flowers will bloom in these months:
   (a) March (b) April (c) August (d) September?
2. What flowers
   (a) grow from a bulb (b) grow from a tuber or winter root?
3. Name three sorts of vegetables that must be planted, rather than sown.
4. What sort of vegetable seed can be sown in (a) February (b) June?

Giving directions

UNCLE BOB IS COMING!

You've never met Uncle Bob before.
He lives in America.
He's rich.
And he's coming to see you.
He's never been to Britain before, and he's never seen a double decker bus.
His plane is bringing him to Heathrow.
He wants to try public transport from there, to see Britain properly.
He knows how to get to your nearest Railway Station.
Send him directions for getting to your home *by bus*.

What he needs to know:
1. Where to get on the bus.
2. What number the bus will be.
3. Where the bus will be going to (destination).
4. What stop to ask for.
5. What special things to look for when he gets off – names of streets, shops, pillar boxes or telephone box.
6. Which way to walk and which way to turn.

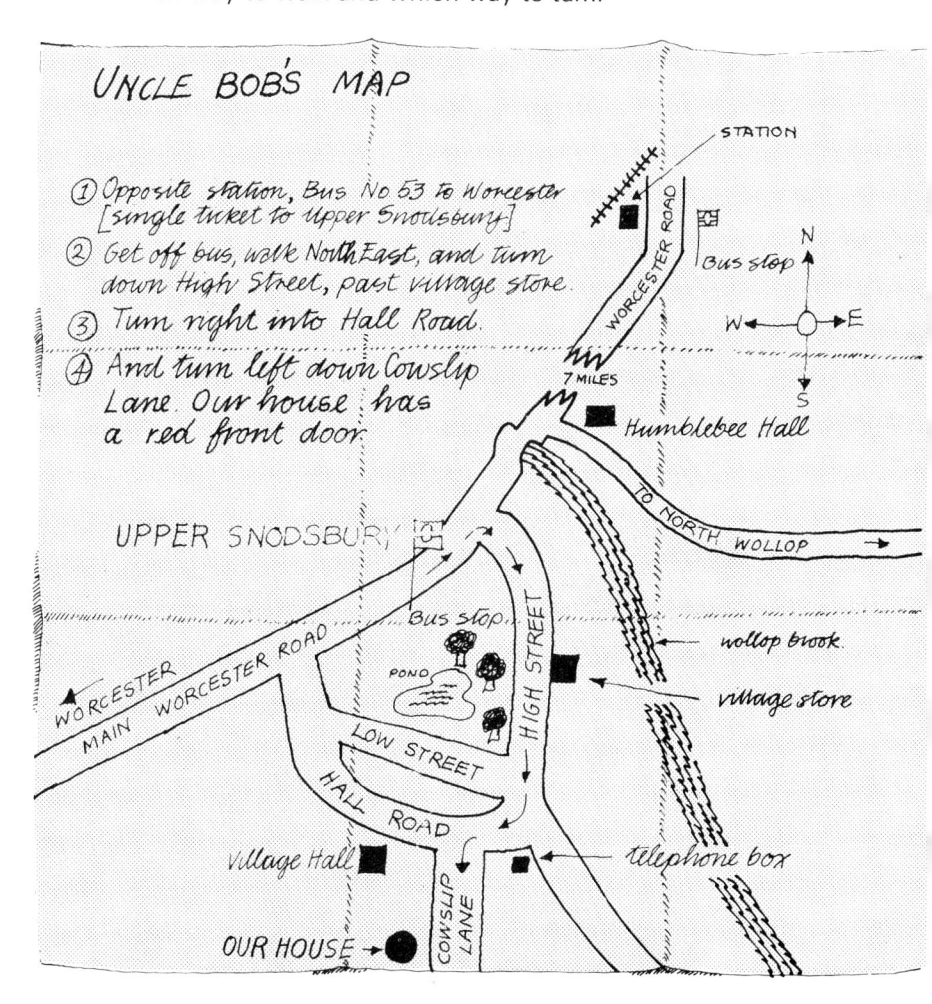

UNCLE BOB'S MAP

1. Opposite station, Bus No 53 to Worcester [single ticket to Upper Snodsbury]
2. Get off bus, walk North East, and turn down High Street, past village store.
3. Turn right into Hall Road.
4. And turn left down Cowslip Lane. Our house has a red front door.

DRIVING DIRECTIONS

Choose a town about 30 miles away from your home that you can only reach cross-country – you can't get there just by going down one main road.

Prepare directions for driving to your home from there. You will need to mention:
- what the road numbers are to take.
- where and which way you should turn corners.
- main landmarks along the route – bridges, rivers, post offices, big buildings.
- how far it is from one corner to the next.

Some of the class are sure to have parents who are members of the A.A. or R.A.C.
Ask at home to see if you can borrow some copies of A.A. or R.A.C. directions from one place to another.
Can you get a copy of the A.A. or R.A.C. route directions from the town you have chosen to your home town?
Do the A.A. or R.A.C. directions put in any bits you left out?

1. Can you explain what these words mean? If not, use a dictionary to help you:
   (a) urban (b) undulating (c) estuary.
2. What are the two words that the driver must look for on signposts, and where will the signposts change from having the first word, and have the second one instead?
3. Can you work out what the abbreviations mean at the point 7 miles from Bristol, where it says (a) rbt (b) SP?
4. Can you explain what the two columns of figures in the margin are telling you?
5. What do the four marks in the black block by the word Michaelwood stand for?
6. What is the driver meant to do at Junctions 13, 12, 11, 9, and 8?

Do what you're told!
Prepare some directions for reaching a place near school. Ask a friend to try them out exactly; do your directions work? Score 10 if they do fit exactly. Lose 3 marks for every mistake, however small it is. Then your friend gives you directions and you follow your friend's route.

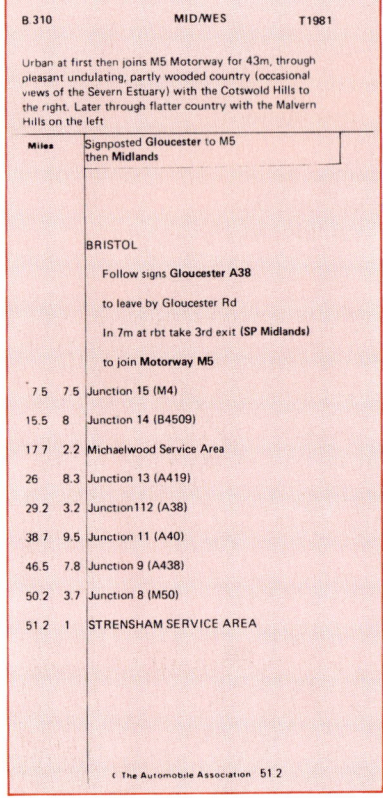

An extract from an A.A. route map

Handling timetables

Timetables for buses and trains look difficult to read – until you know how.
If you are not sure about the 24-hour clock, see page 100.

THINGS THAT MAKE TIMETABLES DIFFICULT

- Some timetables are printed in columns so that as you read down the column you follow the journey. Others are printed in lines so you must read across the page to follow the journey.
- A timetable usually shows all the stops along the route. But the train or bus you catch may not stop at all of these. It may be an express and go through the town without stopping, or one that does not cover the whole route. Stops that are missed will not have a time printed next to them on the timetable.
- A timetable gives a new column or line for each timed journey, but some of these journeys will only be made on weekdays, or on Saturdays, or on Sundays. Look carefully at the top of the page and at the top of the column to see what days that particular column is for. Look at the key to see what letters like SO, SX, or S may mean.
- You may have to change from one train (or bus) to another. Local connecting services may be printed in light print and the main long-distance service in bold print.

If you want to go to Scotland go to bed in London
...on an Inter-City Sleeper

Close your eyes and you're almost there — Inter-City

53

BY BUS OUT OF LIVERPOOL

Look at the Ribble Services timetable printed here and then answer these questions:

1. What is the earliest time you can leave Skelhorne Street bus station for Blackpool?
2. What is the latest time you can leave Skelhorne Street bus station for a through bus to Blackpool?
3. What time would you get to Preston if you left Aintree at 1036?
4. How long does the bus take from Walton, Church to St Annes, Wood Street?
5. If you catch the bus at Ormskirk at 1200, when will you reach Preston?
6. If you stand at the Royal Coaching House, Burscough Bridge, from half past four in the afternoon, how long will you have to wait for a bus to Liverpool?

Liverpool · Preston · Blackpool — TIMESAVER 761

Daily	Code	NSSu	NSu	Su								NSSu										
Liverpool, Skelhorne Street Coach Station	dep	0715	0815		0915	1015	1115	1215	1315	1415	1515	1615	1715	1815	1915	2015	2115	2215	2300			
Walton, Church		0727	0827		0927	1027	1127	1227	1327	1427	1527	1627	1727	1827	1927	2027	2127	2227	2311			
Warbreck Moor, Black Bull		0732	0832		0932	1032	1132	1232	1332	1432	1532	1632	1732	1832	1932	2032	2132	2232	2315			
Aintree, Old Roan		0736	0836		0936	1036	1136	1236	1336	1436	1536	1636	1736	1836	1936	2036	2136	2236	2318			
Maghull, Northway, Jct. Eastway		0742	0842		0942	1042	1142	1242	1342	1442	1542	1642	1742	1842	1942	2042	2142	2242	2323			
Ormskirk, Bus Station	arr	0757	0857		0957	1057	1157	1257	1357	1457	1557	1657	1757	1857	1957	2057	2157	2257	2335			
Ormskirk, Bus Station	dep	0800	0900	0900	1000	1100	1200	1300	1400	1500	1600	1700	1800	1900	2000	2100	2200	2300	2335			
Burscough Bridge, Royal Coaching House		0816	0916	0916	1016	1116	1216	1316	1416	1516	1616	1716	1816	1916	2016	2116	2216	2316	2351			
Rufford, Hesketh Arms		0820	0920	0920	1020	1120	1220	1320	1420	1520	1620	1720	1820	1920	2020	2120	2220	2320	2355			
Tarleton, Cock and Bottle		0827	0927	0927	1027	1127	1227	1327	1427	1527	1627	1727	1827	1927	2027	2127	2227	2327	0002*			
Much Hoole, Smithy Inn		0832	0932	0932	1032	1132	1232	1332	1432	1532	1632	1732	1832	1932	2032	2132	2232	2332	0007*			
Walmer Bridge, Liverpool Rd./Hall Carr Ln.		0835	0935	0935	1035	1135	1235	1335	1435	1535	1635	1735	1835	1935	2035	2135	2235	2335	0010*			
Longton, Rams Head		0839	0939	0939	1039	1139	1239	1339	1439	1539	1639	1739	1839	1939	2039	2139	2239	2339	0014*			
Preston, Bus Station	arr	0856	0956	0956	1056	1156	1256	1356	1456	1556	1656	1756	1856	1956	2056	2156	2256	2356	0031*			
Preston, Bus Station	dep	0701	0901	1001	1001	1101	1201	1301	1401	1501	1601	1701	1731	1801	1901	2001	2101	2201	2301			
Freckleton, War Memorial		0717	0917	1017	1017	1117	1217	1317	1417	1517	1617	1717	1747	1817	1917	2017	2117	2217	2317			
Warton, Pickwick Tavern		0720	0920	1020	1020	1120	1220	1320	1420	1520	1620	1720	1750	1820	1920	2020	2120	2220	2320			
Lytham, Clifton Street (Square)		0729	0929	1029	1029	1129	1229	1329	1429	1529	1629	1729	1759	1829	1929	2029	2129	2229	2329			
St. Annes, Wood Street		0737	0937	1037	1037	1137	1237	1337	1437	1537	1637	1737	1807	1837	1937	2037	2137	2237	2337			
Blackpool, Talbot Road Bus Station	arr	0755	0955	1055	1055	1155	1255	1355	1455	1555	1655	1755	1825	1855	1955	2055	2155	2255	2355			

SUNDAY SERVICE WILL OPERATE ON GOOD FRIDAY AND BANK HOLIDAY MONDAYS
FOR TRAFFIC ARRANGEMENTS DURING CHRISTMAS AND NEW YEAR HOLIDAY PERIODS SEE SEPARATE ANNOUNCEMENTS

Code   **Su** — Sunday only   **NSu** — Not Sunday   **NSSu** — Not Saturday or Sunday   — Adjoining or near Railway Station
* — On the 2300 Liverpool — Preston journey passengers may not be picked up after the vehicle has left Tarleton, Jct. Coe Lane/Windgate

FOR ADDITIONAL STOPPING PLACES SEE BELOW

Passenger Restrictions: Leaving Liverpool the first setting down point is Aughton, Royal Oak and entering Blackpool the last picking up point is Warton, Pickwick Tavern. Passengers are not permitted to make local journeys between Preston, Watery Lane, G.E.C. Factory and Preston, Railway Station/ABC Cinema (inclusive).

ADDITIONAL STOPPING PLACES: BLACKPOOL, *Lytham Road/Kirkby Road, Lytham Road opp. Grand Hotel, Lytham Road near Highfield Road, Rawcliffe Street (Lido); **SQUIRES GATE:** Fylde Bus Depot (near Airport), Pontins Holiday Camp, **ST. ANNES,** St. Thomas' Church, **ANSDELL,** Fairhaven Hotel, **WARTON,** R.C. Church; **FRECKLETON,** Brookfield Residence, **PRESTON,** Watery Lane, G.E.C. Factory, The Ship (nr. Polytechnic), ABC Cinema (near Railway Station); **PENWORTHAM,** Priory Lane; **HUTTON,** Anchor Inn; **LONGTON,** Golden Ball; **BRETHERTON,** Toll Bar; **BURSCOUGH,** Red Lion Hotel; **ORMSKIRK,** County Road/Scott Drive, **AUGHTON,** Royal Oak; **MAGHULL,** Alt Garage; **WALTON,** Hospital; **EVERTON VALLEY,** Walton Road.

* Throughout the period of Blackpool Illuminations this request stop will be observed in Bloomfield Road near the junction with Lytham Road on the following journeys:
1910, 2010, 2110, Blackpool — Liverpool
1615, 1715, 1815, 1915, 2015, 2115 Liverpool — Blackpool

A HOLIDAY TRAIN TO THE WEST COUNTRY

The O'Connor family live in Hartlepool. They decided to travel to Penzance by train for their holiday on 10 September.

a What time did they need to catch the train on the Friday evening?

b Where did they have to change trains, and what time was it?

c What time did they reach Penzance? Which day was it?

Total Reservation Services

		FRIDAYS					SATURDAYS		
		C H	C H	C	C	C	A ✕ ⟁	B ✕ ⟁	
astle	dep	17 58	—	21 00	22 10	—	—	08 35	09 11
m	dep	17 49	—	21,54	22 29	—	—	08 54	09 28
nderland	dep	17 14	—	21 24	21f39	—	—	07 19	08 19
rtlepool	dep	17 42	—	21 53	—	—	—	07 47	08 47
ingham	dep	17 52	—	22t04	—	—	—	07 59	09 01
ockton	dep	18 03	—	22 16	—	—	—	08 10	09 12
gton	dep	18 32	—	22 20	22 56	—	—	09 18	09 49
arborough	dep	17 53	—	21k13	—	—	—	08 07	—
fract Baghill	dep	19 20	—	23 19	23 49	—	07 13	07 25	10 18	10 32
	dep	19 46	—	—	—	—	07 41	—	10 46	10 57
dford Exchange	dep	18 08	20 27	21 27	—	23 14	07 00	07 40	10 02	—
w Pudsey	dep	18 16	20 35	21 35	—	—	07¶11	07 48	10¶10	—
eds	dep	18 42	20 56	22 28	—	23 47	07 36	08e10	10 40	—
kefield Westgate	dep	19g10	20g47	22g56	—	00 06	07 55	08p28	10 58	—
thorpe	dep	—	—	—	—	—	07 52	—	10 57	11x10
n on-Dearne	dep	—	—	—	—	—	08 04	—	11 09	11x24
ll	dep	17 38	19 08	—	—	23 25	06 13	—	09 35	09 35
ssle	dep	17 32	19 16	—	—	—	06 21	—	—	—
rby	dep	17 38	19 22	—	—	—	06 27	—	—	—
ugh	dep	17 52	19 28	—	—	23●38	06 33	—	09 49	09 49
ole	dep	18 09	19 51	—	—	23●55	06 56	—	10 07	10 07
orne North	dep	—	20 01	—	—	00t05	07 06	—	—	—
ncaster	dep	19 14	20 27	—	—	00 39	07 43	—	10 39	10 39
xborough	dep	19 29	20 42	—	—	—	07 56	—	10 53	10 53
erham	dep	20 19	21 35	00 10	—	01 07	08 16	08 58	11 21	11 38
ield	dep	20 38	22 50	00a35	—	—	08 43	09 19	11 43	11 57
terfield	dep	20 56	23 23	—	—	—	09 02	09 35	—	—
ol Temple Meads	arr	00 16	03 10	03 46	04 41	04 49	—	12 42	—	15 03
ston super Mare	arr	—	—	—	06 50	06 50	—	—	16 11	—
water	arr	—	—	—	07 15	07 15	—	—	16 56	—
on	arr	—	04 27	—	06 00	06 09	—	13 38	—	17 13
on Junction	arr	—	—	—	07 58	07 58	—	—	—	—
r St Davids	arr	—	05 12	—	06 37	06 47	—	16 24	16 32
nstaple	arr	—	07 20	—	08 22	08 22	—	19 05	19 05
mouth	arr	—	06 19	—	07 32	07 32	—	17 39	17 39
ish	arr	—	05 33	—	06 54	07 06	—	16 41	16 51
mouth	arr	—	05 40	—	07 01	07 13	14 30	16 47	16 57
on Abbot	arr	—	05 51	—	07 17	07 30	14 42	16 58	17 09
rquay	arr	—	06 12	—	07 32	07 45	14 55	17 11	17 23
gnton	arr	—	06 20	—	07 40	07 53	15 03	17 18	17 31
es	arr	—	—	—	—	08 00	—	17 44	17 44
outh	arr	03 20	—	06 48	—	08 35	14 28	18 18	18 18
ard	arr	04 04	—	—	—	09 12	15 04	20 05	20 05
oe	arr	—	—	—	—	09 48	16 05	—	—
in Road	arr	—	—	—	—	09 25	15 17	20 19	20 19
vithiel	arr	—	—	—	—	09 31	16 37	—	—
wquay	arr	—	—	07 50	—	09 39	15 28	—	—
ustell	arr	—	—	08 42	—	11 12	16 46	22c44	22c44
	arr	04 37	—	08 21	—	09 48	15 38	20 36	20 36
	arr	05 02	—	08 43	—	10 07	15 59	20 56	20 56
lmouth	arr	06 24	—	10 14	—	—	17 09	21 24	21 24
uth	arr	05 22	—	08 59	—	10 22	16 31	21 11	21 11
orne	arr	—	—	09 06	—	10 29	16 38	21 18	21 18
e	arr	—	—	09 16	—	10 38	16 47	—	—
th	arr	05 39	—	09 21	—	10 42	16 28	21 29	21 29
Ives	arr	06 12	—	10 00	—	11 12	17 07	22b12	22b12
ance	arr	05 55	—	09 33	—	10 59	16 40	21 42	21 42

Other Services

	F			SATURDAYS			
		✕ ⟁		⟁	✕ ⟁	D ⟁	E ⟁	✕ ⟁
dep	19 30	08 08	—	11 58	12 17	—	14 00	16 28
dep	19 53	08 14	—	12 15	12 35	—	14 17	16 45
dep	18f39	07 19	—	10f56	11f39	—	12f56	15f39
dep	18 23	07 47	—	11 46	11 46	—	13 46	15 45
dep	18 35	07 59	—	11 58	11 58	—	13 58	15 57
dep	18 46	08 10	—	12 09	12 09	—	14 09	16 08
dep	20 21	08 43	—	12 37	12 57	—	14 38	17 09
dep	20 00	07 55	—	12 13	12 13	—	14n35	16 18
dep	21 34	09 26	—	13 20	13 40	—	15 31	17 54
dep	22 05	—	—	13 03	—	—	—	—
dep	21 02	08 44	09 07	11 55	—	14 00	14 27	17 08
dep	21 10	08 50	09 15	12 05	—	14 08	14 35	17 16
dep	21 42	09 16	09 50	12 40	12 40	14 43	15 02	17 38
dep	22g11	09g08	10 07	13g08	13g08	14g29	15 20	17 57
dep	—	—	—	13 15	13 15	—	—	—
dep	—	—	—	13 26	13 26	—	—	—
dep	19 08	08 25	—	12 32	12 32	13 08	14 23	16 38
dep	19 16	08 06	—	12 40	12 40	—	—	16 46
dep	19 22	08 12	—	12 46	12 46	—	—	16 52
dep	19 28	08 39	—	12 51	12 51	13 21	14 37	16 57
dep	19 51	08 56	—	13 08	13 08	13 37	14 55	17 16
dep	20 01	09 06	—	—	—	13 46	15 05	17 26
dep	22 17	09 33	—	13 39	13 39	14 36	15p46	17 56
dep	22 33	09 46	—	13 52	—	—	14 51	16p01
dep	22 43	09 58	10 37	14 04	14 04	15 04	16p14	18 35
dep	23 22	10 29	10 53	14 24	14 43	15 36	16 34	18 57
dep	23 43	10 28	11 10	14 41	14 41	15 53	16 51	—
arr	04 34	13 38	14 16	17 34	17 46	19 00	20 06	22 05
arr	06 50	14 28	14 42	—	18 44	—	20 30	20 55	23 10
arr	07 15	16 56	16 56	—	—	—	19 36	21 21
arr	06 00	14 58	—	18d21	18 34	—	19 51	21 37
arr	07 58	—	—	—	—	—	20 11	22 56
arr	06 25	15 36	—	18d58	19 08	—	20 30	23 15
arr	08 22	17 05	—	—	—	—	21 35	21 35
arr	07 32	16 39	—	—	—	—	20 48	22 17
arr	06 42	—	—	—	—	—	19 51	20 54
arr	06 48	—	—	—	—	—	19 57	21 00
arr	07 01	16 09	—	19d23	19 36	—	20 56	23 50
arr	07 17	—	—	19d37	20 21	—	21 45	—
arr	07 25	—	—	19d45	20 28	—	21 50	—
arr	08 00	—	—	—	—	—	21 12	—
arr	08 35	16 58	—	—	20 22	21 45	—	00 38
arr	09 12	17 39	—	—	22 01	—	—	—
arr	09 48	18 15	—	—	—	—	—	—
arr	09 25	17 53	—	—	22 15	—	—	—
arr	09 31	18 32	—	—	—	—	—	—
arr	09 39	18 07	—	—	—	—	—	—
arr	11 12	19 00	—	—	—	—	—	—
arr	09 48	18 29	—	—	22 32	—	—	—
arr	10 07	18 53	—	—	22 52	—	—	—
arr	—	19 39	—	—	—	—	—	—
arr	10 22	19 06	—	—	23 07	—	—	—
arr	10 29	19 13	—	—	—	—	—	—
arr	10 38	19 39	—	—	—	—	—	—
arr	10 42	19 24	—	—	23 22	—	—	—
arr	11 12	19 41	—	—	—	—	—	—
arr	10 59	19 38	—	—	23 35	—	—	—

Total reservation of seats is not applicable to trains shown in the columns headed Other Services

ugh services in bold type, connecting ser- in light italic figures. Please ask at your st Inter-City station or British Rail travel t for full details of changing points and times.

⟁ Leeds to Plymouth
⟁ from Leeds
assengers may alight at Bristol Temple Meads to purchase refreshments.
z from Sheffield E ⟁ to Birmingham
ridays only
uns until 5 September
eserved seats may be occupied from 23 30 n Friday
y bus from St. Erth Railway Station

c By bus from St. Austell Railway Station
d Until 6 September
e Through train until 6 Sept On 13 Sept., connecting services dep Leeds 08 21, Wakefield Kirkgate 07 51
f Change at Newcastle
g Wakefield Kirkgate
j Change at York   k From 4 July
n Until 6 Sept On 13 Sept dep 14 11
p Until 6 Sept On 13 Sept dep Doncaster 15 33, Mexborough 15 46, Rotherham 15 58
● Passengers joining at Brough and Goole should obtain reservation tickets from Hull

§ Passengers joining at Thorne North should obtain reservation tickets from Doncaster
† Passengers joining at Billingham should obtain their reservation tickets from Stockton
x Passengers joining at Moorthorpe and Bolton-on-Dearne should obtain their reservation tickets from Pontefract Baghill
¶ Passengers joining at New Pudsey should obtain reservation tickets from Bradford Ex
✕ Restaurant service of breakfast, lunch, afternoon tea, high tea or dinner (according to time of day) for the whole or part of journey
⟁ Buffet service of drinks and cold snacks available for the whole or part of journey

1. The Disney family live in Bradford. They want to spend their holiday in Exmouth.
   a How long will their journey take if they catch the 2314 train on a Friday evening?
   b Could they get any refreshments during the night?
   c Where will they have to change trains?
2. Erika Evans wanted to travel from Wakefield to Sheffield on a Saturday morning. She arrived at the Westgate station at 9.00 o'clock, and phoned Duncan to tell him to expect her at 10.29. But he had to wait until 10.53 before she got there. What had she done wrong?
3. Rodney James lives in Taunton. He set off during the afternoon of Saturday 10 September to catch the train for Newton Abbot. He thought he was going to arrive at 1923 but he was thirteen minutes late. What had he forgotten to notice?
4. Sandy Hamilton was travelling on the 0736 from Leeds to Truro on a Saturday. He enjoyed his breakfast and lunch in the restaurant car on his through train, but when he went to get his tea he was disappointed. What had he forgotten to notice?

TIMETABLES FROM YOUR HOME TOWN

Now look up some of the timetables from your home town. See if you can get copies of:
- local bus services
- long distance coach services
- trains from your nearest station

Choose a place on the timetable with a name beginning with S.
a How many services are there to it each day?
b What is the earliest service?
c What is the fastest service?

WHERE CAN YOU GET TO?

1. Trace a map of your part of Britain, and show on it the places you can get to *on direct services* out of your local town. Use different colours for local buses, coaches, and trains.
2. How can you get from your home to the centre of London? (Londoners: How can you get from London to Carlisle?)
3. What special offer tickets are available from your home district by bus or train? When do you   (a) set off   (b) arrive there   (c) leave there   (d) return home on these special excursions?
4. If there is a real journey you are planning to make soon, try phoning for details of the timetable (see page 46).

The Highway Code

You are going along . . .

Obtain a copy of the Highway Code and answer the following questions (the numbers in brackets are clues that will help you find the answers).

1. You are going along – walking – on a country road in the dark. Make a note of three things you should be careful about. (2)

2. You are going along – walking – and you need to cross the road. There are cars parked along the kerb. What should you do? (21)

3. You are going along – walking – and you want to cross the road at some traffic lights. What three things should you watch? (16)

4. You are going along – driving – at 30 m.p.h. and six lengths behind the car in front, when somebody overtakes you and cuts in in front of you. What should you do? (47)

5. You are going along – driving – when you see a bus stopping. What two things should you do? (51)

6. What is it dangerous to do near animals in the road? (63)

7. You are going along – driving – on a three lane single carriage way. What is the middle lane for? (73)

8. You are going along – driving – and you see a box junction just ahead of you. When can you drive onto it? (92)

KNOWING THE ROAD SIGNS

1. Write down why the drivers in the following six pictures ought to be stopped.

2   What is the difference in law between a round sign, a triangular sign and a rectangular sign?
3   Make neat drawings of the road signs for these things:
    a no through road
    b national speed limit applies
    c 40 m.p.h. limit
    d give way
    e school
    f double bend
    g road narrows
    h stop
    i continuation sign, 40 m.p.h. limit
    j no overtaking
4   What do these signs mean?

5   What are the signs for these things?
    a roundabout ahead
    b slippery road
    c roadworks
    d no parking or waiting
    e steep hill down, 1 in 7
    f dual carriageway ends

STOPPING DISTANCES

1. How many car lengths does it take a car to stop at (a) 30 m.p.h. (b) 50 m.p.h. (c) 70 m.p.h.?
2. If a driver is tired and takes twice as long as usual to react, how many car lengths would it take him to stop at 50 m.p.h?
3. The roads can become very greasy when the first rain falls after a long dry spell and this can double the actual stopping distance. How many car lengths would it take the driver to stop at 50 m.p.h. under these conditions?
4. If the driver is tired (doubling his reaction time) and the roads are wet (doubling the stopping time), how many car lengths would it take him to stop at 50 m.p.h.?
5. Roughly how many feet are there in a metre?
6. Find crossroads near your home or school, and measure out points (a) 75 ft (b) 175 ft (c) 315 ft, from the corner, which show the shortest stopping distances for a car at different speeds. What is the limit at that spot?

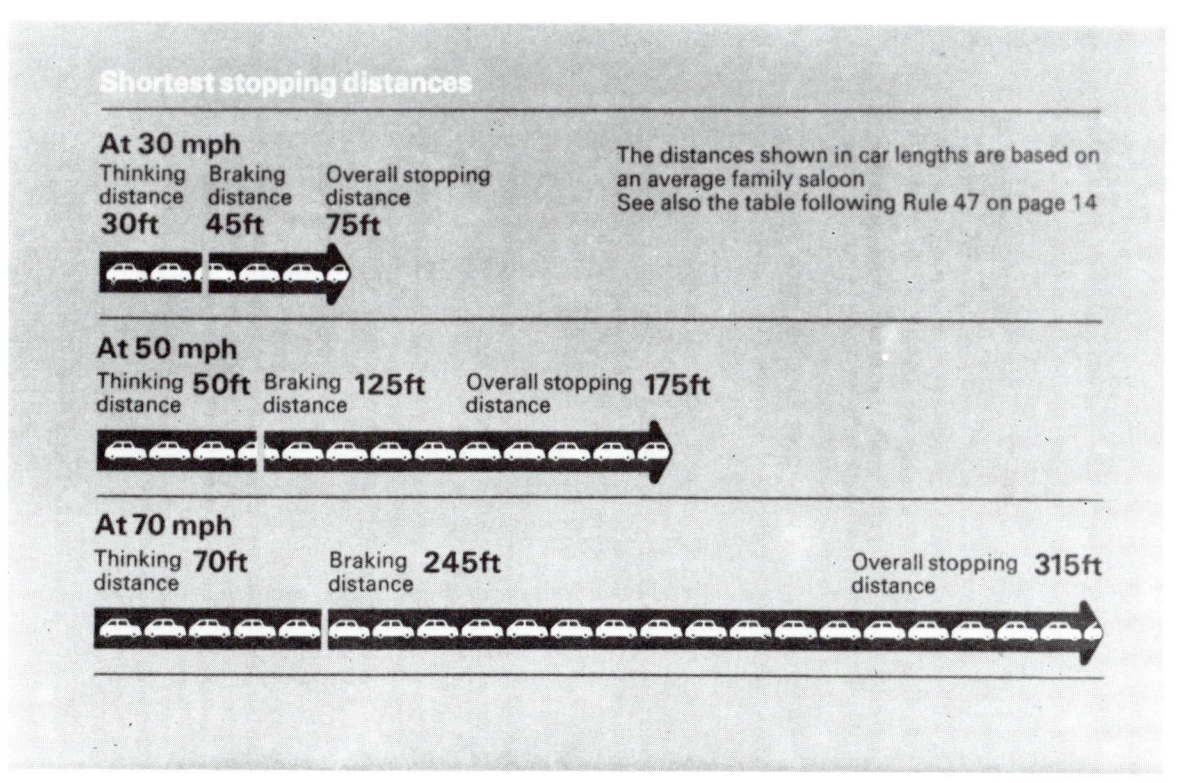

Shortest stopping distances

At 30 mph
Thinking distance **30ft** — Braking distance **45ft** — Overall stopping distance **75ft**

The distances shown in car lengths are based on an average family saloon
See also the table following Rule 47 on page 14

At 50 mph
Thinking distance **50ft** — Braking distance **125ft** — Overall stopping distance **175ft**

At 70 mph
Thinking distance **70ft** — Braking distance **245ft** — Overall stopping distance **315ft**

SURVEY YOUR AREA

How many different road signs are to be found in your home area? Where are they?

A QUIZ

First you must read any parts of the Highway Code that you have not yet read.
Then with the book closed, working in teams of two, see who can score best at this quiz:

1. If you want to walk across the road, what should you do before you step into the road?
2. What should you wear or carry on country roads after dark?
3. When do you have priority at a zebra crossing?
4. What does it mean if the picture of the green man in the traffic light begins to flash?
5. What must a moped rider wear?
6. What should you do if others want to overtake you while you are riding or driving along?
7. How fast can you go along a road with street lights if you can't see the speed limit signs?
8. What does it mean if there is a single broken line, with long markings and short gaps, in the middle of the road?
9. What should you not do while you are being overtaken?
10. Name six different types of places where it is dangerous to park.

WHO'S BREAKING THE RULES?

A small group should go out and watch the roads near school for a little while.
Make a list of all the rules that you see being broken by drivers, riders and pedestrians.
Which are the Highway Code rules that are broken most often in your district?
What dangers arise when these rules are broken?

MAKE A POSTER

When you have found out the Highway Code rules that are broken most often in your district, make a poster for display in school to encourage others to do better in future.
See page 68 for ideas on how you can set out the lettering.

Holidays abroad

Travel Agents will:
- help you choose a good holiday in Britain or abroad
- make the arrangements for you
- get your foreign money and all your tickets
- arrange any journey in Britain.

But you don't have to book through a Travel Agent. You can phone to find out the details yourself, and make your own bookings.

CHOOSING A HOLIDAY

| charter | package | courier | bed and breakfast |
| inclusive | surcharge | tariff | full board |

What do these words mean? If you don't know, read the answers given below and match the right words to the right answers.

- A price that includes all the things you have to pay for.
- A price that covers the cost of all your meals and a bedroom in a hotel or guest house.
- The fare that is right for that time of year, day of the week and time of day – many fares vary from one sailing or flight to the next.
- Someone who is sent by the holiday firm to travel with the party and sort out all the problems along the route.
- A special arrangement for a complete holiday including all the travel and the hotel bookings.
- Extra money that you have to pay and that was not included in the first bill.
- A special arrangement (often with an airline) to carry a load of passengers at a low price.
- A price that covers the cost of your bedroom and your breakfast in a hotel or guest house.

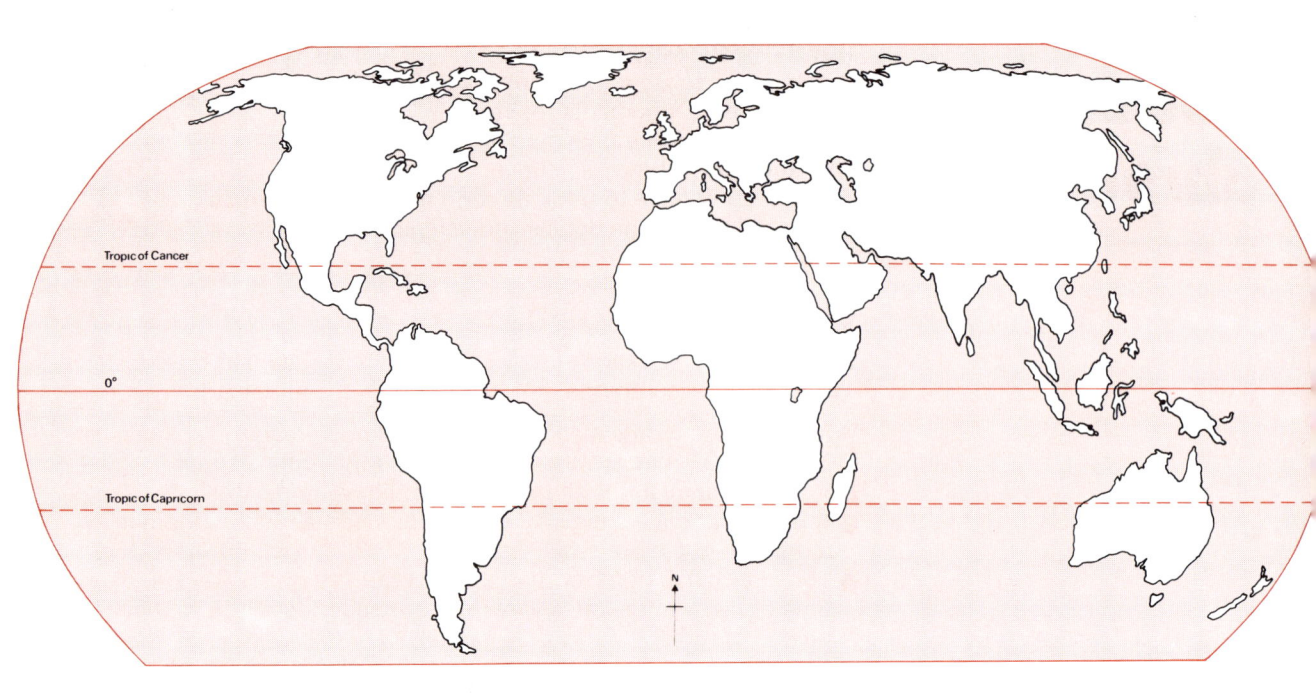

WHERE TO GO

1 Trace the world map on this page.
2 Collect details from your local travel agents for as many different holidays as possible.
3 Mark on your map where you can go and what it would cost.
4 Mark fares along the route and mark prices for inclusive holidays at the place you get to.

WHERE HAVE YOU ALL BEEN?

Members of the class may well have been to many foreign countries, either on holiday or while parents were working abroad. Compare notes on as many different countries as possible. You could make a point of comparing these things:
a the best food you had
b the most exciting thing you saw
c the thing you liked best about the weather
d the happiest day you had there
e special things to buy
f the day you will never forget.

SOME OF THE SIGHTS TO SEE IN THE WORLD

These twelve pictures show some of the famous sights in the world. Identify what they are, and set out your answers in a table like this:

No.	Name of sight	Country it is in	Do you know anyone who has seen it?

Names (not in order)
The Tower, London, England
Eiffel Tower, Paris, France
Leaning Tower, Pisa, Italy
Empire State Building, New York, U.S.A.
Taj Mahal, India
Acropolis, Athens, Greece
Grand Canyon, Arizona, U.S.A.
Red Square, Moscow, U.S.S.R.
Koala bear, Australia
The Pyramids, Nile Valley, Egypt
Kilimanjaro, Tanzania
Inca remains, Lake Titicaca, Peru

63

WHAT ARE YOU LETTING YOURSELF IN FOR?

If you book a holiday through a travel agent you may be letting yourself in for spending more than you think. Particularly if something goes wrong.

Read the small print (probably at the back of a booklet) and see what the conditions of booking really are. Here is a table showing what cancellation charges you let yourself in for if you book a holiday with one of the big agents. Study the table and work out how much the people named in the questions below would have to pay in the end.

Cancellation charges

More than 42 days before start:	lose advanced booking fees £10.00 per person
28–42 days:	25%
14–27 days:	50%
1–13 days:	75%
Day of start:	100%*

Accommodation charges

	9 Apr 22 May	23 May 18 July	19 July 31 Aug
Simple	£5.00	£8.00	£11.00
Super	£6.00	£10.00	£12.00
Luxury	£8.00	£12.00	£15.00

*Please note that insurance against cancellation can be obtained under Gold Cover Holiday Insurance.

1. Lee and Kirsty booked in the luxury accommodation for the period 1 to 10 August but then cancelled on 28 July. How much did they lose?
2. Nigel, Marcus and Ashley booked in the simple accommodation for the period 1 to 14 May, but then were unable to go and cancelled on 1 April. How much did they lose?
3. Anthony and Camilla booked in the super accommodation for the period 1 to 30 June, but then decided to go to Egypt instead, and forgot to cancel their booking. How much did they have to pay?

IS INSURANCE WORTH THE MONEY?

You can buy insurance for your holiday.
If certain things go wrong you will get some money paid to you. But there are other things that could go wrong. If these are not included in the policy you will not be able to claim any compensation whatsoever.

If you want to take out the following insurance it will cost you £1.00 for each day of the holiday, or £10.50 for a whole month.
- You're killed. Your nearest relation gets £3 000.00.
- You're so badly hurt you can *never* work again. You get £3 000.00.

- You die (of disease, not accident). Your body will go back to England free of charge – but no money will be refunded for the return ticket you are not using.
- You cancel the holiday. You will have the cancellation costs paid if you have cancelled because of illness (which means a doctor signs to say it was impossible to go – not just a cold!), or if there is a strike, or the plane or ferry breaks down.
If you cancel for other reasons – too bad, you pay the cost of cancellation (and the insurance).
- If your luggage is damaged or lost (not merely scratched, worn and torn), you can claim up to £500.00.
- If you lose some money, and report it at once to the police and insurance company, you can claim up to £125.00.

No money back if you are pregnant before you start, or ill from some complaint that a doctor has treated you for during the last six months, or if you go motorcycling or take part in winter sports. (You can have another, more expensive insurance for these).

1. Helen dropped her purse with £150.00 in it, but did not notice it until the next day, and did not go to the police till she got home. How much insurance money did she get?
2. Hilary broke an ankle before she was due to go and needed to keep very still. Cancellation charges were £135.00. How much insurance money did she get?
3. Herbert had an accident and lost the sight of one eye which meant he had to give up his job. How much insurance money did he get?
4. Just as the Hughes family were about to set off there was a big fire at their home, and they could not leave the town. They had to cancel on the final day. They had cancellation charges of £843.00 between them. How much insurance money was paid to them?

Holiday money

When you go abroad you need the money of the country you are going to. You can buy the money at:
- a travel agent
- or at the port or airport
- or from a bank
- or from the same sort of place abroad.

You may prefer to buy travellers' cheques and change them when you need them.
You buy the money at the *rate of exchange*.
The travel agent or banker will sell it to you at one price.
He will buy back money you have not spent at another price.
The difference is his profit.

The value of the pound is "floating".
This means that it may change from day to day.
So the price of the foreign money may change from day to day.

What is it now? You can find the answer from a bank, a travel agent, or from many newspapers (not Monday's).

This was the exchange rate on 2 May 1979:

Belgian Francs	62.50 = £1.00
Danish Kroner	10.98 = £1.00
French Francs	9.03 = £1.00
German Marks	3.93 = £1.00
Italian Lire	1 751.00 = £1.00
Dutch Guilders	4.26 = £1.00

If you had gone on holiday on 2 May 1979, and taken £100.00 with you to the airport to change, (a) how many of these would you have got then and (b) how many would you get now?
1 French Francs
2 Dutch Guilders
3 Danish Kroner
4 Italian Lire

If you had just bought £50.00 worth of foreign money, how much (a) would you have got in May 1979 (b) today?
5 in Belgian Francs
6 in German Marks
7 in French Francs
8 in Dutch Guilders

If you had about £80.00 worth, how much would you have got (a) in 1979 (b) now,
9 in French Francs
10 in German Marks
11 in Dutch Guilders
12 in Danish Kroner?

THE CUSTOMS OFFICER IS WATCHING YOU!

In some countries there are limits to the amount of cash that you can take in or out.
In Britain we have strict controls about not bringing animals into the country. Since the British Isles are cut off from the continent by the sea, we have been able to avoid having diseases like rabies here. If someone brought an animal – even their pet – into the country and it developed rabies after it got here, other animals here might catch the disease, and it might spread among wild animals. After this it would be impossible to wipe it out and many new rules and restrictions would have to be made for people with pets.

TRAVELLERS' CHEQUES

If you buy travellers' cheques, you can change them into the foreign money of your choice when you need it, and take them with you to change in any one of many countries.
You can often change them in hotels, as well as big railway stations, banks, travel agents and ports and airports.

You sign them once when they are first given to you. Then you have to sign them again before they can be used. If one is stolen or lost no one else can use it, but you must report the loss at once to the people you bought it from (make sure you know their address). If you do this, some time later you will get your money back from the people who sold you the cheque.

If you don't need so much foreign money after all, you can bring the travellers' cheques back and change them back into British money.

COINS OF THE WORLD

Members of your class are likely to have travelled to several foreign countries, and some may have collections of coins from many countries. Coin collecting can be an interesting and skilled hobby. What can you find out about it?

Layout

Most things look much better if they are well laid out. This chapter gives ideas for layout of notices and posters. See page 162 for laying out letters, page 113 for tidying up your handwriting, and page 70 for layout on a typewriter.

The important thing about layout is to begin by making a plan.
- What are you going to write?
- What are the important headings?
- How much space is it all going to take?
- What size paper have you got?

Tidy layout usually means that what you have put down covers the bottom of the paper at least as much as the top, and the right hand side as much as the left hand side. Letters on one line should usually be all of the same sort and general size (e.g. capitals, italics, small letters or joined letters).
Colour may need to be balanced as well. 'Strong' colours like black and red will not balance well against 'weak' colours like yellow, pink or pale green.

1. How big should the letters be?
   Big enough to stand out, but small enough for the words to fit in easily.
2. How do I begin?
   By writing a rough draft.
3. Where do I begin?
   Not at the beginning, but in the middle of each line, and work outwards from there.
4. How do I know what letter will be in the middle?
   Count all the letters in the words, and add one letter for each gap between the words. Halve the total to find the middle of your line.
5. How far apart should the lines be?
   The gaps should be at least twice as high as the letters on the line below.
6. How do I stop the ruler slipping?
   Spread out your fingers along the ruler while you draw the line.

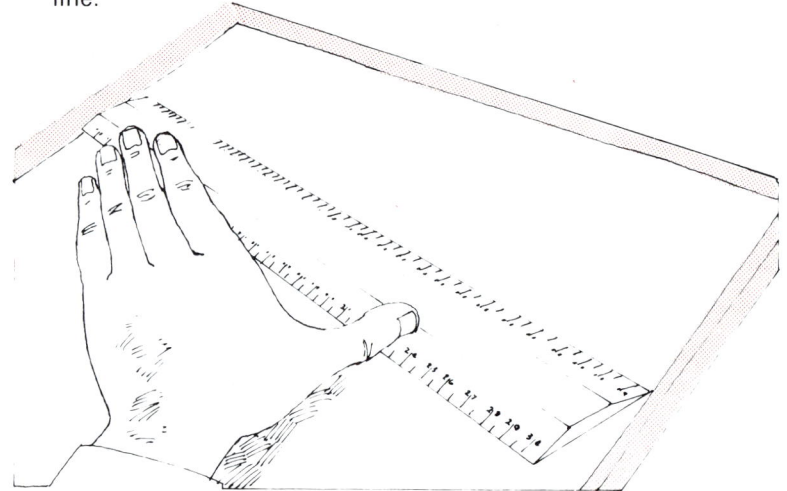

Fishing Competition

BIG PRIZES!

At the Gravel Pits next Saturday
Tickets 20p

FISHING

COMPETITION

BIG PRIZES

At the Gravel Pits next Saturday

Tickets 20p

7   How do I keep the lines level?   (a) Sit up straight and
(b) measure down both the left hand side and the right hand side.

PHOTOGRAPHS

Photographs need attention to layout (or composition) just as much as lettered work. It can look silly to have a picture where the people are right on the edge, and if they are looking out of the picture, you wonder what they were looking at.

1   Bring in some family snapshots. How could they have been improved by better composition?

Do you like these three photographs? If not, how would you improve on them?

OTHER PRACTICE WORK

2   Make a poster of your own either with these words or with others of a similar sort:
   a   Come riding! Horse riding club meets every day. 2.00 p.m. in the pony field.
   b   Our team needs your support. Travel in the team bus free. Every Saturday at 9.00 a.m.
3   Plan the layout of a title page for a topic, such as a section of your Skills work.

Layout on a typewriter

Many people have a typewriter at home. You can learn to use it as a touch typist. You will probably want to take a special course to become good at this. Or you may just want to be able to type something to make it look good and to be able to keep a copy, but not to make your living typing all day long.

Typing can be a good idea for:
- sending orders through the post;
- writing business letters, such as complaints;
- writing to the tax inspector, or about other money matters;
- writing letters to organise things, like a committee meeting.

It is not such a good idea for:
- applying for a job (some employers prefer to see the applicant's handwriting; others may not mind);
- some friendly letters (they can look rather formal: what do your friends prefer?).

Here are some of the things to remember when you are setting things out on a typewriter:

1. Make sure the paper is straight. Use the release lever to free the sheet, and square up the corners before you begin. Clip back the lever, and roll down to where you want to start.
2. If you are using carbon paper, make sure it is the right way round. The black side will face you as you roll it in at the back of the typewriter, and then will be away from you as it comes up ready for being typed on.
3. Plan your margins and move the margin-set positions, and plan your line spacing. Words that are typed often take less room than words that are handwritten, so start far enough down the page so that it does not look silly. But don't put the lines too far apart – this can look messy.
4. Hit the keys with a sharp hard tap – don't press them like an electric button. (Electric typewriters do not need such a hard tap as manual ones).
5. Allow one space between each word, using the space bar at the bottom of the keyboard. Allow two spaces after a full stop or question mark.
6. New paragraphs usually begin either three, or five, spaces in from the margin. Decide which you prefer, and keep to it.
7. Line up new lines that do not go up to the margin, for example the lines on an address. All typewriters have some form of marker to show you where the next letter will be typed.
8. Capital letters, and the different symbols appearing on the top line of the top row (", £, @, & and so on), are obtained by holding down the shift key, which can be found in the bottom corners of the keyboard, while you type the letter you want.

TRY YOUR HAND AT SOME TYPING

1 Make exact copies of the letter and the agenda shown here.
2 When you have done these, try to plan and lay out similar copies of this agenda:
Sports Committee Meeting, 28 February.
43rd meeting to be held in the Sports Hall Office at 6.00 p.m.
AGENDA   1 Apologies for absence.   2 Minutes of the last meeting.   3 Hire charges.   4 Replacement snooker table.   5 Changing room and showers.   6 Use by outside groups.   7 Any other business.
3 Try setting out on the typewriter your answers to other sections of this book. Suitable passages would be:
  a Gardening: The tools for the job
  b Going on holiday: Sights to see in the world
  c Sickness in the family: How to kill germs
  d Trade Unions: Union words
4 Try to make up your own business letters and then lay them out well on the typewriter.

```
                              'Birds-Eye-View
                              22 Dinsdale Drive
                              Gillingham
                              Kent
                              HE7 1YZ

13 February 1983


Dear Sir/Madam,
              Order No. O-NO-999

       I bought this camera from you a month ago
and I have just had my first film processed. It
seems there must be something wrong with the lens:
it is giving a distorted picture.

       I am enclosing one of the prints so that you
can see the sort of thing that is wrong. All my
pictures have come out like this, which is very
disappointing.

       I would be grateful if you could repair or
replace the camera. I have wasted a roll of film
that cost me £2.50 and processing that cost £4.00,
as well as the postage on this parcel (£1.10).
Would you be willing to refund these additional
expenses of £7.60 altogether?

              Yours faithfully,

              I.B. Slim

              I.B. Slim



Post + Buy P.L.C.
Fiddle Lane
Presston-under-Hand
Lincs.
```

```
              SOCIAL COMMITTEE


                  A G E N D A


       for meeting to be held in the Common Room
              at 8.00 p.m. on February 1st


       1.  Apologies for absence.

       2.  Minutes of the last meeting.

       3.  Cost of meals in the cafeteria.

       4.  Equipment in the Common Room.

       5.  Unpaid subscriptions.

       6.  Date of next Disco.

       7.  Installation of new coffee machine.

       8.  Any other business.
```

Locating in alphabetical order

Can you say the alphabet backwards? It's a great help to be able to go backwards as well as forwards if you want to find your way quickly in a long alphabetical list. It can be easier if you have learnt the alphabet in bits, like this:

A B C   O P Q
D E F   R S T
G H I   U V W
J K L   X Y Z
M N

Thousands of lists are printed in alphabetical order.

This means that:
- All words that begin with **a** are put before those that begin with **b**, and so on.
- All the words that begin with **a** are sorted out on their second letters – words that have **b** for the second letter come before those with **c** as the second letter (*able* before *active*).
- All the words that begin with **ab-** are sorted out on their third letters (*able* comes before *about*).
- The words that begin with **abo-** are sorted out on their fourth letters (*about* comes before *above*).
- And so on, right through the word if necessary.

TIDY THE LISTS INTO ORDER

Can you put these lists into alphabetical order?
1. Eire, United Kingdom, France, Belgium, Netherlands, Federal Republic of Germany, Luxembourg, Denmark, Italy, Greece.
2. London, Birmingham, Glasgow, Liverpool, Sheffield, Manchester, Leeds, Edinburgh, Belfast, Bristol, Coventry, Bradford.
3. tyre, tube, tape, valve, valve cap, cotter pin, chain, reflector, saddle, light, brake, bell, spoke, pump, mudguard.

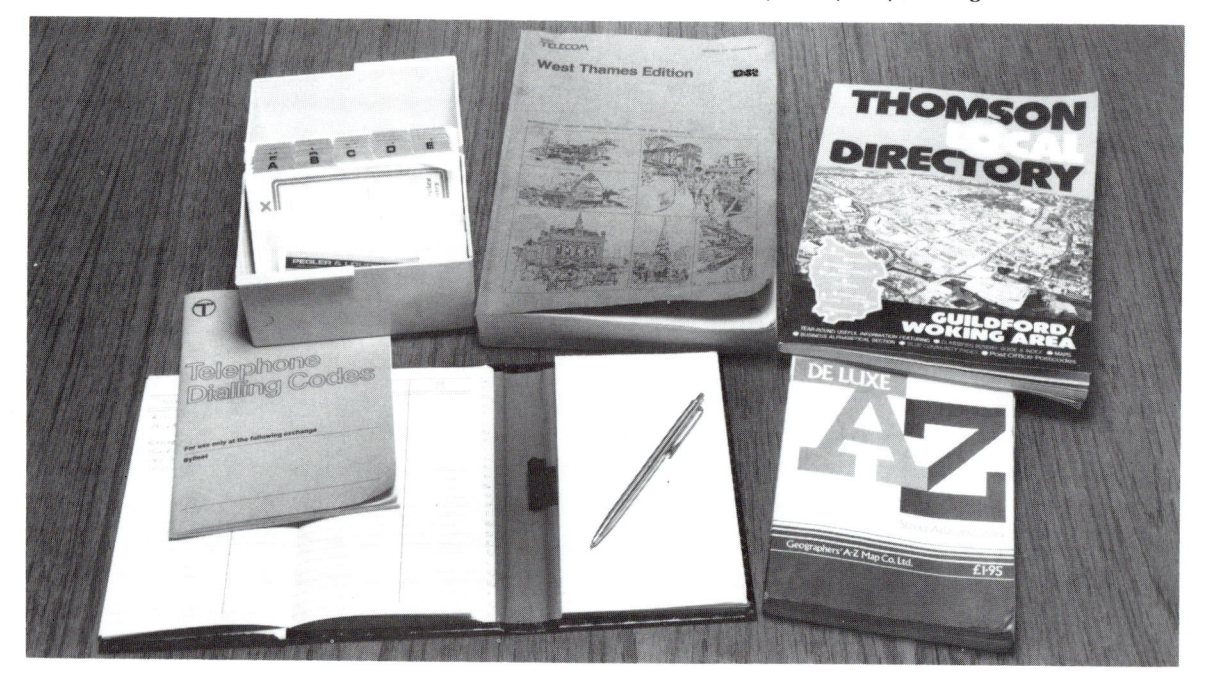

KEEP UP WITH THE JONES'S!

In a phone directory you may find a lot of people have the same name – it might be JONES. When this happens they are listed in the alphabetical order of their first initial (or second initial), and if necessary also their address.

4 Can you put the Wrights in order?
   Wright, T.A.; Wright, L.D.; Wright, A.; Wright, A.K.; Wright, J.L.; Wright, T.M.; Wright, J.J.; Wright, J.K.

5 Look in your local telephone directory. How many have the names a Jones, O.
   b Jones, Q.
   c Jones, U.
   d Jones, Y.?
   e What first names begin with these letters?

CAP IT!

Work in pairs.
Your partner says a word – any word.
You CAP IT by saying another that begins with the same two letters and yet comes after it in alphabetical order. (Ann says 'cabbage', you say 'carrot'). Your partner CAPS YOURS in the same way. (Ann says 'cattle'); and you cap that ('caution'); Ann caps that with 'caw'; and you can't cap that, so Ann wins that round.

Not allowed:
1 just to add S ('carrot' – 'carrots')
2 words not in the dictionary, including names
3 words you cannot explain.

Time limit:
5 seconds per answer. To make it harder:
a decide that the first THREE letters must be the same
b make it a word that comes BEFORE it in the dictionary.

Looking things up

There's an answer you want.
You've got two problems –

ONE: what book to look in.

TWO: how to find it in the book.

A book to look things up in is a **Reference Book**. People don't usually read every page of a reference book. A library of reference books is a **Reference Library**. You must look at the book in the library – you can't borrow these books, but you can be sure they will be there when you want them.

Among the useful reference books are these:
- Dictionaries
- Atlases
- Enyclopedias
- Car manuals
- Telephone directories
- Recipe books
- Home medical reference books
- The A.A. Members' Handbook.

There are thousands of books in a good reference library. Some of these will be books about gardening, home repairs, and hobbies. Others will be very technical ones – ones that can help an architect design a bridge, for example, or an antique dealer find out about his goods, or an athletics coach check the regulations of each sport. There will also be a wide range of journals that come out once a week or once a month with up to date information for people in all walks of life.

MICROFILM AND MICROFICHE

A lot of information is kept these days on microfilm or microfiche. The librarian will help you find out how to use these if you need them. In both cases the idea is that thousands of words can be photographed and printed in tiny writing on to an acetate sheet like a negative. When you want to read it, you put it in a special sort of projector and read what you want on a screen.

Many libraries also provide television information services such as Ceefax and Oracle.

FINDING WHAT YOU WANT IN A BOOK

If you're not sure how to use alphabetical order, see page 72.

Most reference books are rather fat, and you only need information from one page.
You are most likely to find what you want listed in the INDEX.

An INDEX is usually at the back of the book. If you can't find the word you want, think of another word that might have been used for the same thing –

(in a Mail Order Catalogue):
   you can't find "mugs"
   try "cups" – not there
   try "crockery"– yes, page 115.

or words coming in another order:
   you can't find "table mats"
   try – "mats, table" – yes, page 118.

The book may begin with a TABLE OF CONTENTS. This is useful to give you a general idea of what sort of information is in the book. It is less suitable for finding a particular fact.

Encyclopedias

Sometimes the information you want is found in a big block of print. You will do best NOT to read every word, but to SCAN the block of print for what you want to know about. Then read every word of the bit that matters to you.
You SCAN by trying to spot your "key word" as you flick your eyes quickly along the lines. When you spot it, stop and read.
If the block of print has margins set at different points you should be able to find the subsections easily.

Use any volume of any encyclopedia:
1 What is the question?
2 What is the title of this volume?
3 What words do you try in the index to find it?
Write down all the ones that didn't work as well as the word and page number that did.
4 What is the answer to the question?
5 What was the section heading where you found it?
6 How many different margins were used on that page?
7 Look back to the TABLE OF CONTENTS. What was the chapter, (or section, or part) called, that you have just used?
8 What sort of other information can you expect to find in this volume of the encyclopedia?

REFERENCE LIBRARIES

When you go to a reference library you can expect the librarian to be very friendly and helpful. He or she will usually help you find the right book to look up what you want to know.

Useful books in a central reference library include:
Who's Who: It tells you a bit about the life of many of the people who have important or well-known jobs in Britain.
Kelly's Street Directory: It tells you the names and addresses of the people in your town. Not all towns have a Kelly's.
Register of Electors: This lists all the people on the electoral roll, which means most of the people over 18 who were living in the town when the list was last drawn up.
Whitaker's Almanack: A book full of facts and figures about Britain and the world.
Keesing's Contemporary Archives: An up to date history book, with a new chapter added every week, to do with the latest events all over the world.
Oxford Dictionary of Place Names (and Dictionaries of Surnames) – early records of well known names.

SAMPLING THE LIBRARY

Go to a reference library and try to find the answers to these questions. If you cannot find the exact book that is named, set yourself a similar question that can be answered from a book that the library has got on the same topic.

1. Describe the costume of men and women anglers in the year 1788. (Use: Cunnington and Mansfield, *English Costume for Sports and Outdoor Recreation*, publ. A & C Black. Dewey 391).
2. Describe what you can see in one or two of the colour pictures of the Moon's surface. (Use: Murdin and Allen, *Catalogue of the Universe*, publ. Cambridge University Press. Dewey 522).
3. What is special about Hermaness? (Use: Berry and Johnston, *Natural History of Shetland*, plate 9, publ. Collins. Dewey 574).

4 What happens to the colour of an eel when it is in breeding condition? (Use: Newdick, *Complete Freshwater Fishes of the British Isles*, publ. A & C Black. Dewey 597).
5 Where does Dunlop cheese come from? (Use: Eekhof–Stork, *World Atlas of Cheese*, publ. Paddington Press. Dewey 641).
6 What address could you recommend for good food in the area around Inverness? (Use: *Egon Ronay's Lucas Guide*, publ. Ronay. Dewey 647).
7 Who won the Mr Universe title in 1980? (Use: Cook and Marshal, *Guinness Book of Winners and Champions*, publ. Guinness Superlatives. Dewey 790).
8 What special sort of food first came from the Aylesbury area in the eighteenth century? (Use: *A.A. Book of British Towns*, publ. Automobile Association. Dewey 914).

TWENTY QUESTIONS

The answers to these questions are not the sort of thing that you will want to keep in your head. But they are things you may want to be able to find out. How quickly can you find the answers, without damaging the books?

You will need:

A dictionary
A telephone directory
Telephone 'Yellow Pages' or Thomson Directory
Telephone 'Code Numbers' book
An encyclopedia
A medical dictionary
An Atlas
The A.A. Members' Handbook
Whitaker's Almanack

1 What is the dialling code for Ipswich?
2 When were the Olympic Games last held in Britain?
3 What is gastro-enteritis (or gastritis)?
4 How far is it by road from Wolverhampton to Liverpool?
5 Which river flows through Gloucester?
6 When and how was paper first made?
7 Which day is Early Closing Day in Chester?
8 How many A.A. recognised hotels are there in Brixham?
9 What does paraphernalia mean?
10 What is the incubation period for chicken-pox?
11 What country are the Canary Islands governed by?
12 What is the telephone number of your local Department of Health and Social Security?
13 What does impetuous mean?
14 What county is Matlock in?
15 What number do you dial for reporting a fault in a telephone?
16 What firms near your home can supply you with a lorry load of building sand?
17 What is the difference between immigration and emigration?
18 Which areas have a lot of tornadoes?
19 What is lockjaw and how can you prevent it?
20 What are fireballs and where have some landed?

Perhaps you can make up another quiz like this to do with things you want to know about in your own home district.

Money sums

Most people check shop prices carefully.
But do you check the typing onto the till roll?
Cash out assistants can make mistakes.
Mistakes may cost you more than you saved on their bargain offer.

Seymour checked the till roll in the sport shop.
What did he find that was wrong? What should the total be?

sports socks	£1.80
shorts	4.10
swim trunks	3.80
T shirt	3.05

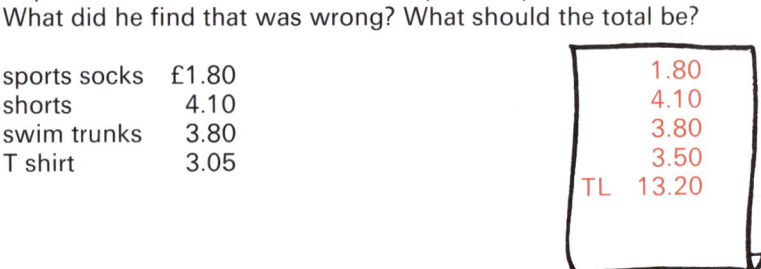

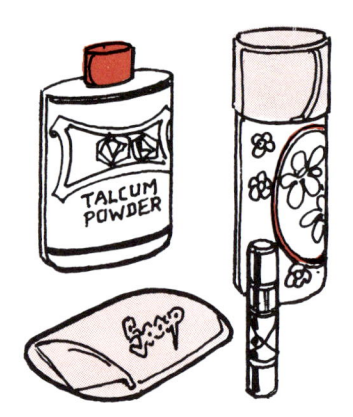

```
        1.80
        4.10
        3.80
        3.50
TL     13.20
```

Seymour told Samantha about the mistake.
So she checked her till roll in the chemist.
What mistake did she find?

talc	0.85
soap	0.48
lipstick	0.72
deodorant	1.40

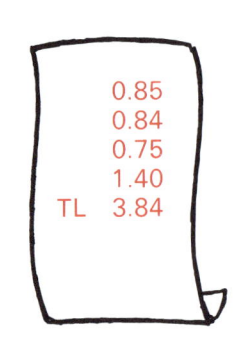

```
        0.85
        0.84
        0.75
        1.40
TL      3.84
```

Seymour and Samantha went to Sabah.
She checked her shopping basket from the Motorists' Centre.
What mistake did she find? What should the total be?

de-icer	0.80
antifreeze	1.50
bulb	0.75
sponge	0.40

```
        0.80
        0.80
        1.50
        0.75
        0.40
TL      4.25
```

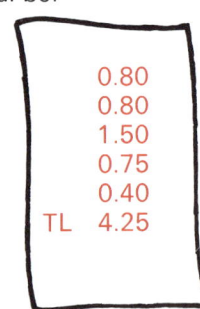

ADDING UP MONEY

Adding up money is just like doing any other adding-up sum.
Remember to keep the numbers in their columns.
How much do these sums add up to?

1	00.37 00.62	5	16.64 10.16	9	49.49 51.51	13	10.05 90.05
2	00.23 00.27	6	105.00 150.00	10	16.27 82.73	14	23.75 23.75 23.75
3	01.56 03.43	7	10.50 10.50	11	14.87 16.56	15	02.04 03.40 01.51 01.25 02.30
4	11.50 15.25	8	09.49 00.51	12	18.88 28.88 16.88		

CHECKING YOUR CHANGE

The change you should get is the answer to a take-away sum:

How much did you pay?	£5.00	
How much you should pay	4.23	Take away
= change	£0.77	

How much change should you get if you pay with a £5 note for each of these bills:

a	£4.50	d	£3.15	g	£1.13	j	£3.68
b	£3.25	e	£2.50	h	£0.25	k	£2.32
c	£3.25	f	£2.25	i	£4.75	l	£2.25

MORE CHANGE TO CHECK

Take each line in this table on its own.
The first and last column should add up to the middle column.
Copy the table and fill in the gaps.

What it cost	What you gave	Change due to you
£1.43	£2.00	_____
£1.43	_____	£3.57
£4.16	£5.00	_____
_____	£4.00	£0.31
£1.52	£1.60	_____
£8.41	£10.00	_____
_____	£8.50	£0.41
£2.67	£3.00	_____

PRICE IT YOURSELF

Do these sums in your head to check that you are not buying potatoes at the same price as peaches.

How much should you pay for these loads of fruit and vegetables?
a 2 kgs of cabbage at 30p per kg.
b 1½ kgs of apples at 54p per kg.
c 2½ kgs of carrots at 42p per kg.
d 6 kgs of potatoes at 24p per kg.
e ½ kg of grapes at £1.80 per kg.

SHORT CUTS

If you want to do the sum quickly in your head it is often quicker to work out how much so many times a 'round' figure would be, and then to take off, or add on, the odd bits. Use 'rounding' to work out these sums:

f 8   kgs of new potatoes at 39p per kg.
g 6   kgs of plums at 69p per kg.
h 5   kgs of cooking apples at 49p per kg.
i   4   kgs of parsnips at 28p per kg.
j   25 kgs of King Edward potatoes at 19p per kg.

COMPUTERS AT THE CHECK-OUTS

More and more shops are using computers at the check-outs. Some of these read the bar-code on the side of a tin or a packet, and then 'look up' the day's price for this item before printing it out on the till roll. Others are used by an assistant who scores through the number in a catalogue to tell the computer what to supply.

If you are shopping in one of these shops all you have to do is to look up the catalogue number of what you want and put it on the order form. The assistant will then price and total it for you. But if you do the pricing and totalling too, you can check that it is right.

Using the information given here, complete the order forms for these goods, price and total them:

Vladimir bought:
Slazenger Squash
   Racquet
Vinyl Sports Holdall
Leather football

Vanessa bought:
Dunlop Tennis Racquet
Slazenger Tennis Balls
Sports shoulder bag

Vivienne bought:
Badminton
   Starter Set
Carlton
   Shuttlecocks
Adidas Sports
   Bag

SHARE THE COST

Your friends promise to share the cost.
But how much is their share?
These are just ordinary division sums.
Be careful to keep the pounds and the pence on their sides of the decimal point.

Example: Four of you share rent costing £37.60

$$4\overline{)37.^160}$$
$$9.40$$

How much must each of you pay here?
a Three of you share petrol costing £9.69
b Five of you sharing a meal bill costing £17.50
c Six of you sharing sports hall charges of £6.66
d Yourself and three friends sharing snacks costing £7.20
e Your brother, sister, and yourself with two friends sharing rent coming to £35.50.
f Frank, Vic, yourself and the twins sharing petrol costing £125.00 on holiday.

THE PAPER SHOP AND THE MILKMAN

Checking some bills means doing some multiplying and some adding. How much do these bills come to?

```
18 daily papers at 20p each     ..  ..  ..  ..  ..  ..
18 evening papers at 15p each   ..  ..  ..  ..  ..  ..
 3 weekly papers at 18p each    ..  ..  ..  ..  ..  ..
 3 magazines at 55p each        ..  ..  ..  ..  ..  ..
                                            Total: £_____

               ..  ..  ..  ..  ..  ..  ..

27 pints of milk at 21p a pint  ..  ..  ..  ..  ..  ..
 4 pots of yoghourt at 18p each ..  ..  ..  ..  ..  ..
 1 pot of cream at 61p each     ..  ..  ..  ..  ..  ..
24 eggs at 85p a dozen          ..  ..  ..  ..  ..  ..
                                            Total: £_____
```

PER ANNUM

Some people's pay is quoted by the year (= p.a., which stands for the Latin words *per annum*), and others by the week. There are 52 weeks in a year.

Who earns most in each of these pairs, and how big is the difference?

(*Hint*: multiply the weekly amounts by 50 and add two more so

£60.00 p.w. × 50 = £3 000
£60.00 p.w. × 2 = £ 120
£60.00 p.w. = £3 120 p.a.)

a Heather: £70.00 a week   Harish: £3 500 p.a.
b Munir: £50.00 a week   Mark: £2 500 p.a.
c Sheralyn: £40.00 p.w.   Louise: £2 100 p.a.
d Nicholas: £75.00 p.w.   Simon: £3 675 a year
e Justin: £100.00 p.w.   Jorg: Annual salary £5 275
f Pavlo: £120.00 weekly   Philip: Salary £5 500 p.a.

MONTHLY INCOME

Many people are paid monthly, while others get a pay packet every week.
Who earns most here, and how much more is it than the others get?

(*Hint*: There are twelve months in a year, so multiply monthly amounts by twelve and weekly amounts by 52, and then you will be able to see how much each person is paid in a whole year).

g
> **WANTED:** Keen young clerical worker Good working conditions Good prospects
> Salary £4 250.00 p.a.

> **WANTED:** Keen young clerical worker Good working conditions Good prospects
> Wages £84.00 a week

> **WANTED:** Keen young clerical worker Good working conditions Good prospects
> Salary £360.00 per month

h Jack, who is getting £310.00 a month
   Jason, who is on £3 750.00 a year
   or Jonathan, who is getting £72.00 a week?

i Lorna (£4 750.00 p.a.), Lynda (£405.00 a month), or Lucy (£95.00 a week)?

j Rona (£5 597.00 p.a.), Rachael (£444.00 a month), or Rebecca (£105.00 a week)?

H.P. PAYMENTS

Sometimes you pay much more for something if you buy it on H.P. than if you pay cash for it. But if you want to know how much more it costs, you will have to do the same sort of sum. How much do these things cost on H.P.?

Example:
            Set of golf clubs: cash down £104.00
                  H.P. Payments: deposit   £26.00
                + 52 weekly payments of £2.00 £104.00
                  Total payment by H.P.   £130.00
                  Saving bought for cash   £26.00

And these? Set out each one like the one above:

What it is	Cash price	H.P. deposit	Weekly payments	Years and months on H.P.	Total H.P. price	Saving bought for cash
New Suit	£88.00	£22.00	£3.00	6 months		
Moped & extras	£750.00	£275.00	£5.00	2 years		
Holiday tour	£220.00	£80.00	£3.50	40 weeks		
Video cassette recorder	£499.00	£175.00	£4.40	$1\frac{1}{2}$ years		

Percentages

Percentages keep coming up in daily life.
Many shopkeepers talk about them.
Unions are always arguing about them.
News bulletins are always full of them.
How do you work them out?

Acme Carpets
final reductions NOW 20% off all stock

MINERS DEMAND 10%

5% of the country UNEMPLOYED!

A SAFE WAY

This way will let you work out any percentage sum there is.
No one can ever set you a percentage sum that will be hard if you do it this way (though they can set *long* sums).
There are other ways and some short cuts that often work.
Start by being sure of the safe way that always works.

Example: 27% of £318.20
Write down the percentage   27

Write the percentage like this:
per goes as a line ... ...   ―――
cent means a hundred   100

Write the word 'of' as ×
Write the total amount on the top line
Therefore the final layout of the sum follows this pattern:

$$\frac{27 \times 318.20}{100}$$

Now multiply the top line:

```
   318.20
      27 ×
  ───────
  2227.40
  6364.00
  ───────
  8591.40
```

= £ $\frac{8591.40}{100}$

And divide the top by 100 by moving two columns across the decimal point = £85.914

This is the right answer, in pounds, but we do not often talk like this, because we usually talk about pounds and pence. So if it is a money sum in a shop we usually round it off to an exact number of pennies – is this case, £85.91. If the answer had been £85.915 we could write £85.91½, and if it had been £85.916 we might round it to £85.92. If it was not money – say it was the amount of nylon in a fabric – we would keep the figures as 85.914 units.

Now try the safe way of working out these sums. Write them in full: don't use short cuts until you are sure of the safe way.

a   12% of £24.00   f   12% of £240.00
b   14% of £31.00   g   14% of £131.00
c   21% of £42.00   h   21% of £412.00
d   21% of £31.00   i   21% of £3 142.00
e   41% of £13.00   j   41% of £3 113.00

k   42% of 31.24 tonnes of scrap metal was iron.
l   24% of 32.41 metres of cloth was damaged.
m   44% of 43.24 litres of shampoo was spilt.
n   70% of 6 550 people went on holiday this year.
o   51% of 327.00 kgs of mushrooms had maggots.
p   42% of 31 240 boxes of oranges went bad.
q   24% of 324 100 letters went by first class mail.
r   44% of 423 400 calves born were female.
s   51% of 703 200 unemployed young people were girls.
t   71% of 565 556 tourists spoke good English.

WHAT A PERCENTAGE IS

The idea of a percentage is that we pretend that we cut up anything we have into a hundred equal parts. We might have a big piece of wood, and cut it into a hundred big equal parts, or a small piece of wood, and cut it into a hundred small equal parts.

If we take five of the hundred big parts, we will have the same share, or fraction, or proportion of the big board, as we have if we take five of the hundred small parts.

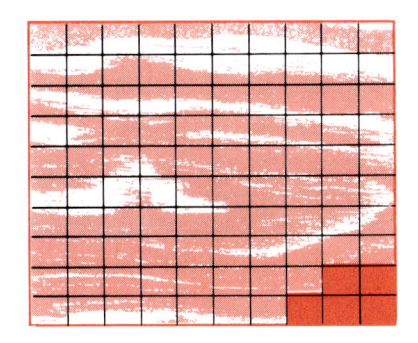

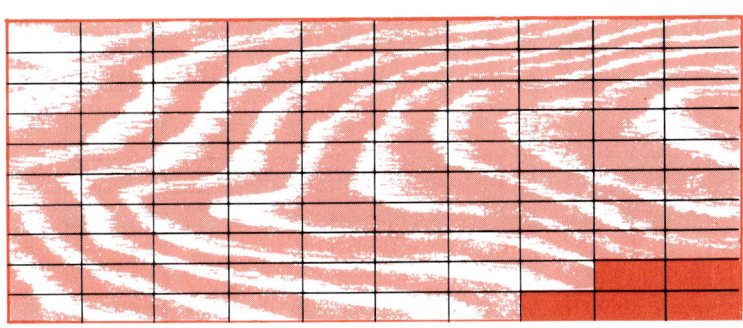

The boss's pay packet may have 100 £5 notes, and if the tax inspector takes 30 of these (= 30%), he will have taken the same share as he does if he takes 30 £1 notes from a worker who gets £100.00 pay.

Draw a set of squares with ten units along each side (cms, or other equal units), and shade the right number of small squares in each big square to mark these percentages on them (in the same way as the artist has done on the next page):

a   10%   f   40%
b   25%   g   60%
c   50%   h   80%
d   75%   i   90%
e   20%   j   99%

LANDMARKS

There are many 'landmarks' on the range of percentages that are the same as well-known fractions. People may keep switching from saying 'half' to 'fifty per cent', or say 'We'll go halves', 'We'll go fifty-fifty'. Add up the shaded squares in these blocks to say how many per cent (%) these common fractions are. (Write the answer like this:

(k) 1 in 4, or $\frac{1}{4}$ = 25%)

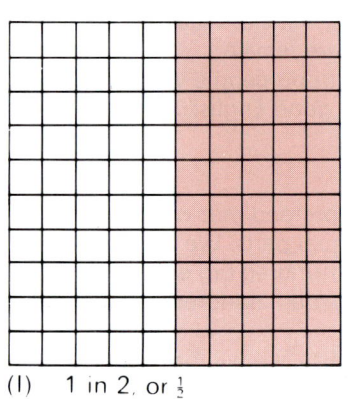

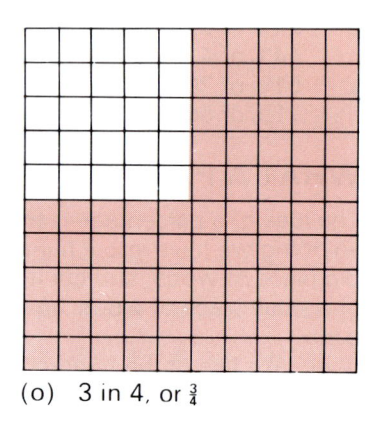

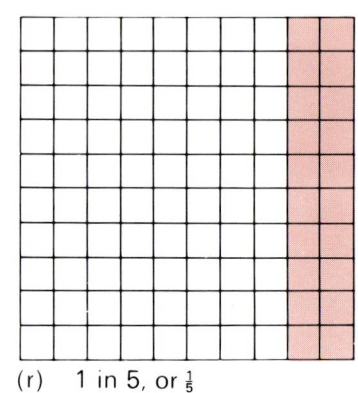

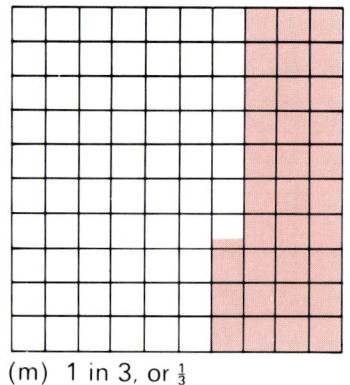

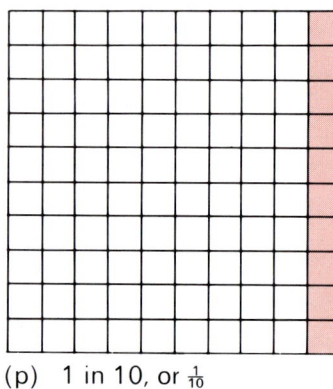

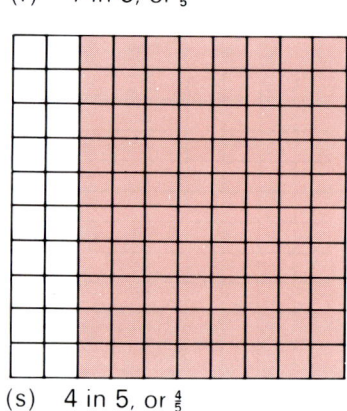

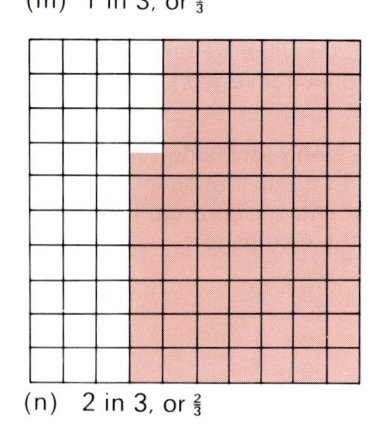

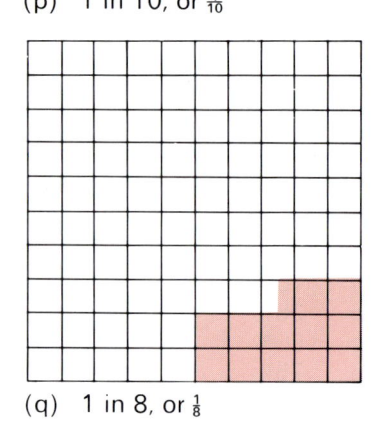

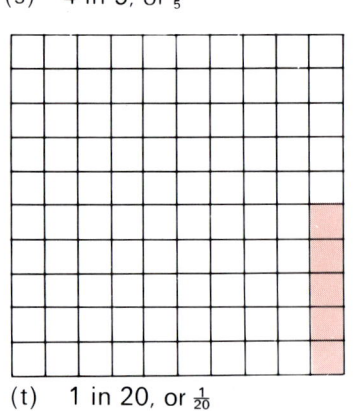

(k) 1 in 4, or $\frac{1}{4}$

(l) 1 in 2, or $\frac{1}{2}$

(o) 3 in 4, or $\frac{3}{4}$

(r) 1 in 5, or $\frac{1}{5}$

(m) 1 in 3, or $\frac{1}{3}$

(p) 1 in 10, or $\frac{1}{10}$

(s) 4 in 5, or $\frac{4}{5}$

(n) 2 in 3, or $\frac{2}{3}$

(q) 1 in 8, or $\frac{1}{8}$

(t) 1 in 20, or $\frac{1}{20}$

86

ANOTHER WAY TO WORK OUT A PERCENTAGE SUM

You might get in a muddle if you learn more than one way to do a percentage sum. The safe way on page 84 is sure to work, but if you have been taught another way in Maths you might prefer to stick to it. This is another way:

Start by dividing the amount by 100
   for example, to calculate 13% of 3.85,
   divide 3.85 by 100 = 0.0385
   then multiply this by the percentage

```
        0.0385
           13 ×
        _____
          1155
          3850
        _____
        0.5005
```

So the answer is 0.5005

Try this method, if you want to use it, on these sums:

a 13% of 4.85　　　　f 34% of 4 132
b 31% of 3.85　　　　g 45% of 2 310
c 23% of 14.2　　　　h 54% of 3 120
d 32% of 41.2　　　　i   65% of 4 154
e 43% of 2 143　　　j   67% of 5 441

Short cuts

10% of something is one tenth of it. So you move ONE digit to the right across the decimal point.

5% is half of 10%, so you start by moving one digit to the right across the decimal point, and then halve the answer.

$2\frac{1}{2}$% is half of 5% or a quarter of 10%, so you either work out 10% and divide by four, or work out 5% and halve it.

30% is three lots of 10%, so you work out 10% and multiply the answer by three.

$37\frac{1}{2}$% can be worked out by finding what 10% is, putting it down three times, and then adding half of 10%, and then half of that (10% + 10% + 10% + 5% + $2\frac{1}{2}$%). That may look a lot on paper, but is not so bad in your head!

Copy out this grid carefully and then fill in the gaps to try out the short cuts:

Question	10% =	Times?	5% =	$2\frac{1}{2}$% =	Answer
10% of £550.00					
$12\frac{1}{2}$% of £550.00					
$17\frac{1}{2}$% of £550.00					
30% of £600.00		× 3 =			
60% of £150.00		× 6 =			

Now try your hand at these discounts.
Shade the squares you don't need to use and then fill the numbers in the others.

Question	10% =	Times?	5% =	2½% =	Answer
12½% of £100.00					
17½% of £200.00					
35% of £200.00					
35% of £400.00					
37½% of £500.00					

PERCENTAGES WITH DECIMALS

Sometimes, for example on pay rises, a percentage may have a decimal point in it.

You work out the sum in just the same safe way as any other percentage sum.

The thing to remember is what to do when you are multiplying by a decimal. That is, to add up the number of digits that are to the right of the decimal in the two lines of the question, and to make sure the same number of digits (including noughts) are to the right of the decimal in the answer.

Example:
Pay rise 8.31% of £47.50

$$\begin{array}{r} 8.31 \\ 47.50 \times \\ \hline 41550 \\ 581700 \\ 3324000 \\ \hline 3947250 \end{array}$$

$$= \frac{394.7250}{100}$$

$$= £3.95 \text{ (rounded)}$$

How much will these pay rises come to?
a 8.5% of £40.00
b 9.3% of £50.00
c 6.8% of £60.00
d 5.25% of £47.50
e 12.5% of £65.75
f 7.75% of £68.75

CHANGING AMOUNTS INTO PERCENTAGES

If you are told that your pay (which is now £53.00 a week) is going up by £5.00 a week, but Bruce's pay (which is now £80.00 a week) is going up by £10.00 a week, you might think that this was not fair. So you would want to know how much each pay rise is as a percentage.

All you do is:
Put the pay rise on top and divide by the old pay

$$\frac{£5.00 \times 100}{53}$$ and multiply it by 100

```
      009.43
53)500.00
    477.    −
    ─────
     23.0
     21.2   −
     ─────
      1.80
      1.59
```

Your pay rise was just over 9.43%

a How much was Bruce's?

And how much are these?
b Betty's rise was £8.00 and her old pay £64.00
c Bernard's pay is now £100.00 and is going up £12.50
d Becky's pay is now £64.00 and is going up £11.50
e Barry's pay is going up £15.00 from £150.00
f Belinda's pay is going up to £96.00 from £84.00.
g Brian's pay is going up to £250.00 from £200.00
h Beryl's pay is going up to £160.00 from £120.00.
i Bradley's pay is going up to £88.00 from £80.00.
j Beverley's pay is going up to £78.00 from £72.00

£1 + 1p = 1% rise

£1 + 2p = 2% rise

£1 + 5p = 5% rise

£1 + 10p = 10% rise

£1 + 20p = 20% rise

£1 + 50p = 50% rise

OPINION POLLS

We are always being told what percentage of people
watch ITV,
would vote Conservative,
earn more than so much,
live in their own homes,
have Building Society accounts,
prefer football to cricket,
prefer tennis to netball,
and so on.

What this means is that some people have been asked these questions and the totals have been converted to a percentage (%). It is easy to forget what a lot of people there may be that make up the 17% or whatever it is that makes the 'minority' group. Complete the blanks on this table:

Question	Total asked	Answering Yes	%	Answering No	%	Total population	Total 'no' would be
Will you go away for your holiday?	314	168		146		56 000 000	
People of Wales, do you speak Welsh?	233	112		121		3 000 000	
Glaswegians, do you work hard at school?	355	295		60		862 000	
Brummagens, do you support Arsenal?	480	45		435		920 000	
Bristolians, have you seen S.S. Gt. Britain?	125	80		45		388 000	
People of Bradford, do you watch cricket?	750	550		200		281 000	

Punctuation

Punctuation is part of saying what you mean in writing. It helps the reader to make sense of what you put down.

THE COMMONEST PUNCTUATION MARKS

Every sentence ends with a full stop. You won't be far out if you say that a sentence is a group of words that makes sense.

1 How many sentences are there in the first eleven lines of black print on this page?

Every sentence begins with a capital letter.
Capital letters are also used for names of people and places. For example, you need them for the following address: Jane Harris, 2 Pilgrims Street, Bath, BA2 3YZ.

2 List the capital letters used since the end of question one under two headings: (a) new sentences (b) names.

Some people, such as journalists, teachers, and authors, make lists of things in their sentences, or make a sentence that is so long, that we need to use a comma, which goes below the line, to show when to take a breath, or pause.

3 How many commas were used in that last sentence?

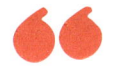

Speech marks (or quotation marks) show which words someone said. For example:
"It's raining," said Dean in disgust.
"Have you brought your umbrella, Maria?" asked Martin.
"Luckily I have," she said, well organised as usual.

4 How many people contribute to this story?
5 Would you recognise a question if it did not have a question mark?
6 Do all questions need answers?
7 Do you think it would be a good idea if we printed a ¿ as they do in Spanish, at the beginning of a question?

91

, We'll do well to remember apostrophes if we haven't put all the letters in. We'll stands for "we will" but it has two letters left out. What's left out of "haven't"?

DON'T put an apostrophe in front of every **s** at the end of a word. "It's" only has an apostrophe if it means "it is".

8 Write out all the words that have been shortened, in their full form.

, The name on the book's cover shows it was Stephen's and not Steven's because he spells his name with **ph** but Steven's name has a **v**.

DON'T put an apostrophe in front of every **s** at the end of a word. You only need it for missing letters or the 'belonging **s**' – Glenn's coat, Zoe's pen, Paul's bicycle, the school's television.

Note It is NOT used with: its, theirs, yours, hers, his, ours.

9 Make a list of all the words in this little section that end with **-s** or **-'s**, under two headings:

the belonging **'s**	other words ending with **s**

! Nearly forgot it! The exclamation mark! What a lot of punctuation marks there are! Thank goodness there's an exclamation mark to warn us about it!

10 What sort of letter is always used after an exclamation mark?

CORRECT THEIR MISTAKES

The pupils who wrote the following passages failed to include their punctuation. Make tidy copies for them with all the punctuation marks in.

> the sport I like most of all is canoeing its great fun going out on fast water sometimes you capsize and thats fun too theres a lot to learn before you are really good at it but its a healthy thing to be doing

> its Bills birthday tonight I wish I had a lovely dress like Janes she only got it the other day and its super

29 kinedale road
carlisle
ca1 1ga

13 november 1983

dear sir/madam

quotation for moped insurance

could you please send me a quotation for comprehensive insurance for a moped i will be 16 in a months time and i would like full cover i will be getting a provisional driving licence the moped i have bought is a second hand one that cost me £350 and i will be keeping it in a lockable garage at this address

yours faithfully
jeremy rider

bigrisk insurance co ltd
4 buck mary anne street
accrington
lancs
bb5 5ne

> 1 april 1983
>
> 8 the folly
> bury
> lancs
> bl9 5ya
>
> dear sir or madam
>   vacancy for school leaver
> could you please send me full details
> of the vacancy advertised in the paper
> this morning for a school leaver to
> train in your circus as a lion tamer
>   i have always been very interested in
> animals and my friends say i have
> a gift for taming them since we
> have had thirteen different stray cats
> come to live in my house and they
> have all become tame so that they never
> bite or scratch i would love to work
> in a circus
>
> 2 savage street   yours faithfully
> bolton   percy mayle
> bl1 1ar

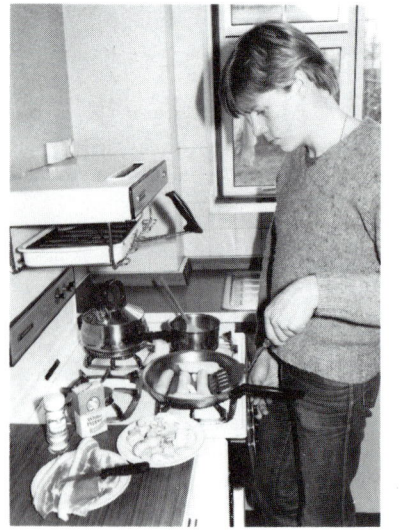

Write out this recipe with the correct punctuation marks:

Sausage Risotto

4 servings
250 gms long grain rice
500 gms pork sausages
150 gms bacon
100 gms mushrooms
fat for frying
¼ teaspoon garlic salt
¼ teaspoon pepper

cook rice until just tender fry the sausages in pan with chopped bacon and sliced mushrooms lift the sausages out stir the cooked rice into the remaining mixture season stir well together pile rice on to hot dish with the sausages along the top a few whole mushrooms can be fried separately and served with the dish

Reading to children

Small children love to have books read to them.
They like to hear the same story time and again.
They like bits that are repeated time and again so they can learn them and join in.
They like to ask all sorts of questions about pictures and words.

Do you sometimes look after small children?
Have you tried reading to them?

It's all very well to be able to read this story page for yourself, but it is not the same to read it to a child. You have to make your voice sound interesting. You have to *tell* the story from the book. You have to read at the right speed. You have to put up with questions and comments. But it is great fun to do.

While you are reading, the child is looking at the pictures. Your eyes are on the words, but you may be asked questions about the pictures. You can understand all the words, but the child may not understand some of them. You have to use your voice to point out the words that matter most. Often these words are names. Or they may be little words like 'he' or 'she' or 'but'.

Sometimes the story will be best read fast; sometimes you will need to say the words carefully and clearly.

1   Which words are repeated more than once in this piece?
2   What three different words all sound much the same?
3   How is the child's interest kept up at the end of the page?

Your answers to all these questions show you bits that need special care when you are reading aloud.

MAKING YOUR VOICE LIVELY

There are three main ways of changing your voice to make a story lively:
- You can puff a tiny bit harder, like when a teacher says '*Don't* make a mess!' We are printing this in italics.
- You can go faster or slower, with pauses in between words, like when you are warned: 'Now—look—here—young—man!' We are printing this with spaces marked in between the words.
- You can raise or lower your voice, usually up for a question or when you are surprised, and down for the end of a sentence or for sad bits. 'Are you hurt? Poor thing!' We are printing these words higher or lower than the rest of the line.

"Well, I really never," said the large
and growly bear to himself.
"There must be someone I can frighten!"
So the large and growly bear
went growling and prowling and scowling,
looking for someone to frighten.
And what did he see?

Now here is the same passage written out again using these rules. Try reading it aloud:

"*Well*, I *really* never,"-—-said the large and growly bear to himself.

"There must be *someone* I can frighten!"

So the large and growly bear

went-—-growling-—-and prowling-—-and scowling,

looking for someone to frighten.

And what did he see?

THE STORY OF BENJE

Here is another story written out in the same way for you to practise:

Benje told him his----sad----story.

"*Who* needs a tail?"----croaked the bullfrog. "*I* had one once and lost it. *Good* riddance, too!"

And later on in the story came the conclusion:

And he found that,----with practice, he could do all the things he could do before,----except swish his tail. But that *really* was not very important.

1. What do you think Benje's sad story was?
2. How did the bullfrog cheer him up?
3. What would you answer if a child asked:
   a "What could he do before?"
   b "What does 'Good riddance' mean?"
   c "What does 'important' mean?"
4. Now try your hand at this sort of reading. Try reading a child's book to a friend in your class, or practise it with a tape recorder. It doesn't matter if you overdo the way you vary your voice at first; you can always make it more ordinary later. It's much better to make it too lively than not lively at all. And when you have practised it enough, try reading it to a child.

Benje told him his sad story.
"Who needs a tail?" croaked
the bullfrog. "I had one once
and lost it. Good riddance, too!"

Reading instructions

At the self-service petrol station.

Directions for use
1 Set indicator on side of pump to blend required.
2 Remove nozzle from holster.
3 Place nozzle in tank fill pipe.
4 Squeeze trigger until required quantity is indicated or delivery stops automatically.
5 Replace nozzle in holster.
6 Check indicator and pay cashier.
If in difficulty contact cashier by pressing signal button.

Dry cleaning at the launderette:

1 Weigh clothes and pre-spot if necessary.
2 Turn pockets and cuffs, close zippers, remove plastic belts, buttons and ornaments.
3 Place clothes in machine, deposit coins, and close door. Door will not lock unless correct amount is deposited.
4 Door unlocks automatically at end of cycle. Remove clothes and hang on hangers.
CAUTION: do not clean rubber, leather, or suede garments.

School fire notice:

If you find a fire ...
Shout "Fire" and keep on shouting.
Break the nearest fire alarm.
Do not try to put the fire out.
WALK quickly to the nearest exit.
Wait just outside until you are sure a member of staff knows exactly where the fire is.
Go to the fire assembly point and join your tutor group.

Power drill instructions:

Instructions for 2-speed drills.
This drill operates at two speeds 900 r.p.m. and 2 400 r.p.m. The speed in engagement is shown on the shift lever when in the closed position.

To change speed
1 Lift the shift lever outwards until it reaches an upright position.
Ensure motor is stationary.
2 Rotate half turn.
3 Snap back to closed position.
4 Rotate chuck half a turn by hand. Alternative speed is now engaged.
WARNING
The speed should never be changed while the motor is running.
Always set speed before fitting unit to any attachment or accessory.

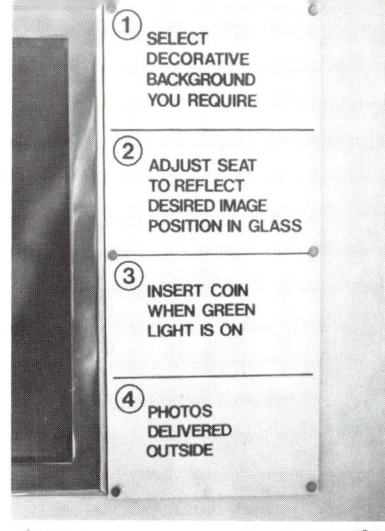

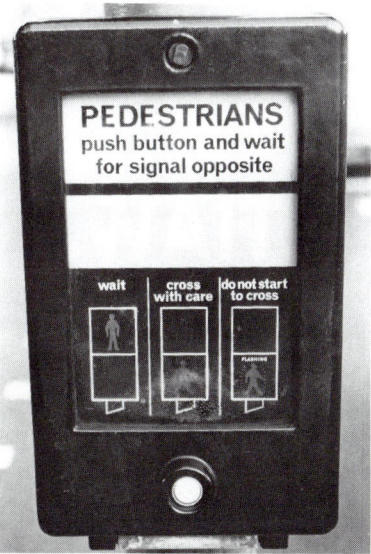

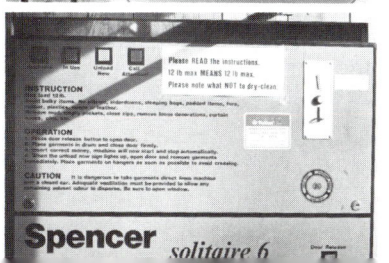

WORDS TO EXPLAIN

Notices often have lots of words in them that are not the words we use in ordinary conversation.
Two particularly important words are

Clockwise   Anticlockwise

1 Here is a list of words in 'notice language' and a list of words 'as we talk'. Pair them off in a neat list.

'Notice language'	Words 'as we talk'
depress	way out, or door
select	push down
CAUTION	a bit that fits on
deposit	choose
insert	work
operate	be careful
accessory	put in
automatically	put down
exit	on its own

2 What notices are around warning you of dangers? Make exact copies of them.
3 What instructions can you find on machines or gadgets? Make exact copies of them if they are not too long.
4 What instructions for your attention are posted around? Make notes of any hard words or unclear instructions.
5 Explain in your own words from the top example on the previous page (petrol station) 'until required quantity is indicated'.
6 Explain in your own words from the second example on the previous page (launderette) (a) pre-spot if necessary (b) deposit coins.
7 See the school fire notice on the previous page. Why does it tell you to WALK away from a fire?
8 Explain in your own words from the power drill instructions (a) speed in engagement (b) ensure motor is stationary.
9 What differences are there in what you would do if you carried out the instructions for a self-service station that are printed on the previous page, or those shown in the photograph on this page?
10 What differences are there in what you would do if you carried out the instructions for a launderette that are printed on the previous page, or those shown in the photograph on this page?

99

Reading the 24-hour clock

There are twelve hours in the morning.
When the afternoon comes the clock has already been all the way round once.
So one o'clock in the afternoon is 12 + 1 which is 13 hrs.
To make it clear that we are talking of the 24-hour clock we don't say 13 o'clock.
Because the time is written 1300 we call it "thirteen hundred hours".
Fifteen minutes later we would write it 1315 and call it "thirteen fifteen".
At one minute to two we would write 1359 and call it "thirteen fifty nine".

1. Two o'clock in the afternoon would be ...... hours.
2. What would half past two in the afternoon be?
3. What would three o'clock in the afternoon be?
4. What would half past six in the evening be?
5. What would eight o'clock in the evening be?
6. What would quarter past eight in the evening be?
7. What would ten o'clock in the evening be?
8. What would 43 minutes past eleven in the evening be?

Has anyone that you know got the 24-hour clock in his watch?
What clocks that you know show the 24-hour clock?
Where is the 24-hour clock used?

A few special points:
- Midnight is called 0000 hours (nought hundred hours), not 2400 hours.
- Noon is 1200 hours (twelve hundred hours).
- We always use four figures, even if it means putting a nought in front.
- A time like 0425 is spoken as "oh-four-twenty-five".
- Every 60 minutes the new hour is clocked up, so that the time is 1400 hours, never 1360 hours.

SHOW YOU CAN DO IT

1 to 12   Write these times down using the 24-hour clock system.

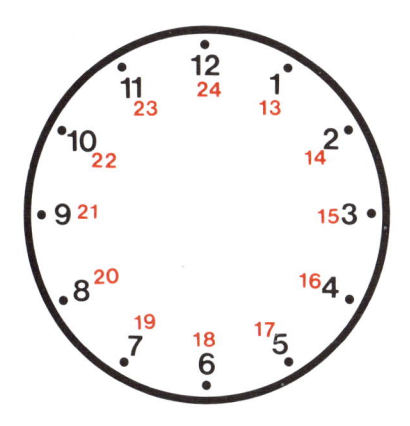

13 to 24   Trace this clock face and put hands onto each of twelve faces to show the times. Remember! The minute hand is longer than the hour hand. The hour hand moves a little between the hour marks as the time goes on.

13	0005	16	0500	19	0930	22	1640
14	0230	17	0630	20	1125	23	1755
15	0440	18	0845	21	1430	24	2000

25   Write out your school timetable for today, using the 24-hour clock all through.

26   Write out the main events of your day from waking until sleeping, using the 24-hour clock all through.

27   Make up a perfect day off, with interesting events at different times, using the 24-hour clock all through.

Sales literature and insurance

Lots of advertisements come through the door.
There are probably envelopes for free film, and publicity sheets from local shops.
And your parents probably get letters they never expected.
Letters that tell them they've won a chance to get a fortune.
Letters that try to sell them things that they never even thought of buying.

Try to collect some of these letters and leaflets.
Bring them to school.
Have a good look at them together. Discuss each of them and write answers to these questions.

Will you get a prize?
- Is there a big prize for someone?
- How many prizes are given altogether?
- How many people do you know who have got the same letter?
- Do you have to send in a "Yes" ticket to win the prize?

BOOK OR GADGET – DO YOU WANT IT?

Until the letter arrived, you had probably never thought of buying that book or gadget. How does the letter try to persuade you to spend money on it?

If you have not had a letter recently answer these questions by looking at the advertisement on the next page for the *New Book of Britain's Roads*.

1. What does it say that makes you want to buy it to impress the neighbours?
2. What does it say that makes you think the outside looks good?
3. What does it say to make you think the people who wrote it or made it are important?
4. Does it say that the pictures or the mouldings are superb, and do they matter?
5. What does it say to make you want to read what is written, or to use the gadget regularly?

IS IT WORTH THE MONEY?

6. How much will it cost altogether when you have added up the first payment, the instalments, and any postage you have to pay?
7. How much would other books or gadgets for the same purpose cost?
8. Will you use it all? If not, how much would the bit you would use cost elsewhere?
9. What would you have done with that money if the letter hadn't arrived?

You need this super

New Book of Britain's Roads

The most important book ever published for the motorist — a work that surpasses in value any other book ever sold.

Claim your copy now.

★ *Give it a trial, free and without obligation. Then it's yours, if you decide to buy it, at a fantastic bargain price just for those lucky people who get this special invitation.*

All you want to know — and things you never thought of!

Super maps printed in lots of colours to help you know exactly where you are, devised specially by the British Institute of Vehicular Studies.

Super route charts to help you plan long journeys, drawn by Bob Freeman and based on his lifetime of experience that has made his name known to millions.

Super guide to all the best resorts by the real consumer experts, the British Hotel Users Association.

Super feature on racecourses and speedway tracks by world-famous speedway driver Alex Armstrong.

Super hints on how to find out what's gone wrong with your car by the Director of Vehicle Repairs in one of Britain's largest car factories.

Super page on roadsigns and route numbers by the Chief Highway Officer of a large County Council.

Super guide to the trees and hedgerows of Britain by Professor C. Andrews.

Super do-it-yourself weather forecasting system by Dr. W. Clarke, internationally famous for his research on meteorology.

Marvellously bound in real leather covers, tough to stand up to heavy wear. Just the right size to fit in your car, 332mm x 240mm. A fantastic 496 pages all yours to examine FREE for ten days — and to keep at the special privilege price.

HURRY! HURRY! HURRY!

If you're one of the first 5,000 people to buy a copy of the amazing NEW BOOK OF BRITAIN'S ROADS you should stand a chance to win one of the THREE NEW CARS we are giving away! Just fill in the coupon and post today!
Send no money now. If you decide to keep the book, it's all yours for £1.85 deposit and three monthly instalments of £1.25.

CEREAL PACKETS

Big packets that catch your eye at idle times like meal times are often used for advertising.
Collect as many different advertisements from packets as you can get.

Make a list of them all like this:

Which packet?	What is offered?	How many packets must you buy?	Cost through packets	Cost in shops	Do I want it anyway?

INSURANCE

You'll want insurance for your moped and later for your car. You may want insurance for your holiday. As soon as you've got a home of your own representatives from different firms may call trying to sell you life assurance. You may have other things you want to insure.

Do you know the meanings of these insurance words? If not, read the answers given below and match the right word to the right answer.

policy	underwriter
third party	quotation
premium	to make a claim
no claims bonus	expiry
broker	liability

- A price that is quoted for you to pay if you decide to take this insurance.
- A legal document on which is printed an agreement between the insurance company and you. It says what you can claim and when they will pay you.
- The need to make a payment by law.
- Someone who is not on one side or the other in an argument: for example in an accident, the passenger in the car which hit you (the driver of the car is the second party and you, riding your moped, are the first party).
- To get in touch with the insurance company and ask for money to be paid to you.
- The end of an agreement.
- Money that you are let off paying because you have not made a claim.
- A sort of shopkeeper who sells you insurance from any of a number of insurance companies; he will suggest a 'good buy'.
- The people in an insurance company who write at the bottom of the agreement that they will make sure you get your money if you have a valid claim.
- The price you must pay every year to keep the insurance.

THINKING ABOUT INSURANCE

1. Look at the photograph of a damaged car on page 13. Which of these people or aspects would be involved after that accident? (a) broker (b) underwriter (c) third party (d) no claims bonus.
2. Use the Telephone Yellow Pages or Thomson Directory to find the names of insurance brokers in your district.
3. Find out details of what the insurance companies or brokers can offer for (a) moped insurance (b) holiday insurance (c) life insurance that might interest you. (If you need to write a letter, look at the model on page 93, but remember to include punctuation).
4. Compare the details of insurance obtained from different companies to see (a) which is cheapest (b) what you get back – which is most generous (c) what restrictions are made in the small print.
5. Look at the advertisement shown on this page. What dangers does the Sun Alliance and London Insurance Co. see in life?

Seeing the doctor

At your age, you may not want to see a doctor for years. But you never know. If you do have to see one
a can you explain what's wrong when you get there
b can you make sense of what the doctor tells you?

WHERE ARE YOU HURT?

Can you be exact about the names of all the parts of the body? Trace this drawing, and label the parts to make sure you know where they all are.

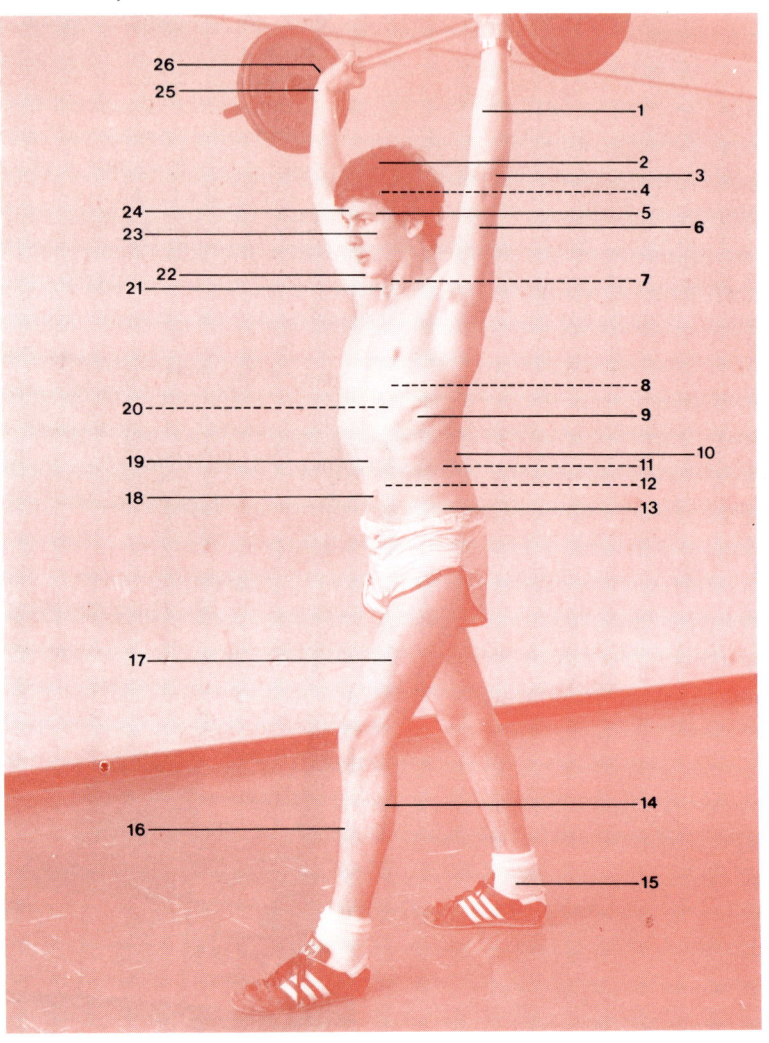

Crown
Skull
Forehead
Temple
Cheekbone
Chin
Upper arm
Elbow
Lower arm

Wrist
Palm
Gullet
Windpipe
Lungs
Ribs
Diaphragm
Navel
Stomach

Intestines
Kidneys
Small of the back
Hips
Thigh
Shin
Calf
Ankle

106

WHAT IS THE MATTER?

Match the right one of these names to the right description.

glands   tendons   cartilage   veins   arteries
muscles   rash   heartburn   colic   migraine   cramp
vomit   diarrhoea   have a temperature   boil   scab
fester   pus   mucus   inflammation

- an area that has turned hot and red
- discharge of a thick creamy fluid, probably from a gland
- yellowish-white fluid from an infected wound or sore
- a cluster of small red spots
- a burning feeling in the lower part of the chest
- sharp pains in the intestine
- very sharp headache and feeling of sickness
- a sudden and painful tightening of a muscle
- be sick
- 'loose tummy'
- having a temperature above 37° C (98.4° F)
- a hard infected swelling
- a hard dry crust formed over a wound or sore
- germs growing and developing in a wound
- organs in the body that make and squeeze out important chemicals
- elastic parts of the flesh that can be tightened or loosened to allow movement
- thick cords that join muscles to bone
- gristle between bones that move, keeping bones apart
- tubes that carry blood from the heart to the limbs
- tubes that carry blood from the limbs to the heart

Speech bubbles:
- Dress the wound twice a day
- It's a bacterial infection
- I'll give you some Antihistamine pills to take
- You must take a laxative
- You need an antitetanus
- It's a virus
- I'll give you some antibiotics to take
- You have dislocated your ---
- Take three tablets four times a day
- Take two tablets every six hours

WHAT DOES THE DOCTOR MEAN?

Look at the things the doctor has been saying, shown on these pages in balloons. Which of these does he say when:

1. He has treated you for a dog bite?
2. He has treated you for a burn that needs a new bandage (or dressing) twice a day?
3. You have pulled a bone out of place without breaking it?
4. He wants you to take some tablets at regular intervals, even waking up during the night to take them?
5. He wants you to take some tablets at breakfast, lunch, tea and bedtime?
6. He is talking about an illness like 'flu or the common cold?
7. He is talking about an illness like some tummy troubles, a sore throat or a boil, that is caused by bacteria?
8. He is giving you some medicine that can kill living germs like bacteria?
9. He is giving you something to make your tummy better when you are constipated?
10. He is giving you something to work against the histamine poisons in your bloodstream?

BOOKS TO LOOK UP

There are a lot of medical books on the market. They help some people. They worry other people, who always think they have something wrong with themselves. If they worry you, don't use them. But you may need to look at them a bit before you know whether they will help you or not. Have a look at these for a start:

A Dictionary of Symptoms by Dr. J. Gomez (Paladin)
Family Health Guide (Reader's Digest)
Family Medical Dictionary by Dr. T. Weston (Hamlyn)
Baby and Child Care by Dr. B. Spock (Bodley Head).

1. What do the books say you should do about:
   - a a wasp sting
   - b migraine
   - c an epileptic having a fit
   - d a burn
   - e a sore throat
   - f constipation
   - g mouth ulcers
   - h eczema
   - i athlete's foot
   - j toothache, when the dentist isn't there

2. Discuss together how much use medical books are, for the ordinary home.
   Are any of the books you have seen worth having at home? What problems could arise as a result of having these books around?

Sickness in the family

If someone in the family is unwell, you should collect some information before you phone the doctor.
The doctor may want to know if the patient has a temperature. Find out before you phone.

HOW TO TAKE A TEMPERATURE

- Kill any germs on the thermometer by putting it in a glass of diluted disinfectant, like Dettol – you need only a small spoonful of the disinfectant in the glass. Then fill it up with cold water.
- Shake the thermometer downwards with a sharp flicking movement. (Make sure you do not hit anything!) Clinical thermometers have a narrow neck that stops the mercury going back into the bulb when the thermometer is taken out of the mouth. The idea is to shake the mercury back into the bulb so you can take a new reading.
- Read the thermometer to make sure you have the mercury down below 36.5° C (or 97½° F) before you begin.
- After about 1½ minutes, read the temperature. If you find it difficult to see the mercury column, turn the thermometer slowly until a corner on the glass acts as a magnifying glass and shows it up.

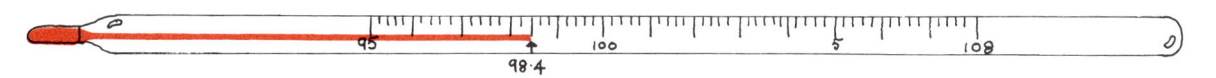

1. Take the temperatures of all the members of your group. Are they all the same? 'Normal' temperature is around 37.0° C (or 98.4° F). Is there anyone with a temperature above 37.5° C (99.3° F) or below 36.5° C (97.5° F)? If so, is he or she well enough to be in school?
2. What do these words mean? (a) concussion (b) fainting (c) dislocation (d) fracture. The doctor may ask about them if the patient has fallen over.
Use medical books to look them up and make short notes.

The London Hospital - Alexandra Wing

3 If the patient has any form of cut or graze, an antitetanus may be needed. Look this up and explain what it is.
4 The patient may not seem too bad, and you may decide to try to look after him or her yourself and not to call the doctor straight away. The photograph shows the things that any home should have in a first aid box and some additional medicines that can be useful. Which of the things shown in the photograph would you use for these patients?
  a Gary is the baby, only about a year old. He keeps crying, and clearly has stomach ache.
  b Gillian is four. She has just had a cold and now has a bad cough that hurts a lot.
  c Geoffrey is seven. He has just come in after falling over on the pavement. He has grazed his knee, cut his hand and bruised his elbow.
  d Gaynor is ten. She has just been in the garden and sat on an ants' nest.
  e Gordon is fourteen. He has just come home from a game of basketball where he slipped and sprained his ankle badly. It is causing him quite a bit of pain.
  f Gail is seventeen. She is suffering from a very bad headache, feels dizzy and sick and won't eat anything.
  g Uncle George is feeling liverish and uncomfortable, and keeps complaining of indigestion.
  h Aunt Grace has aches and pains in her legs and back.

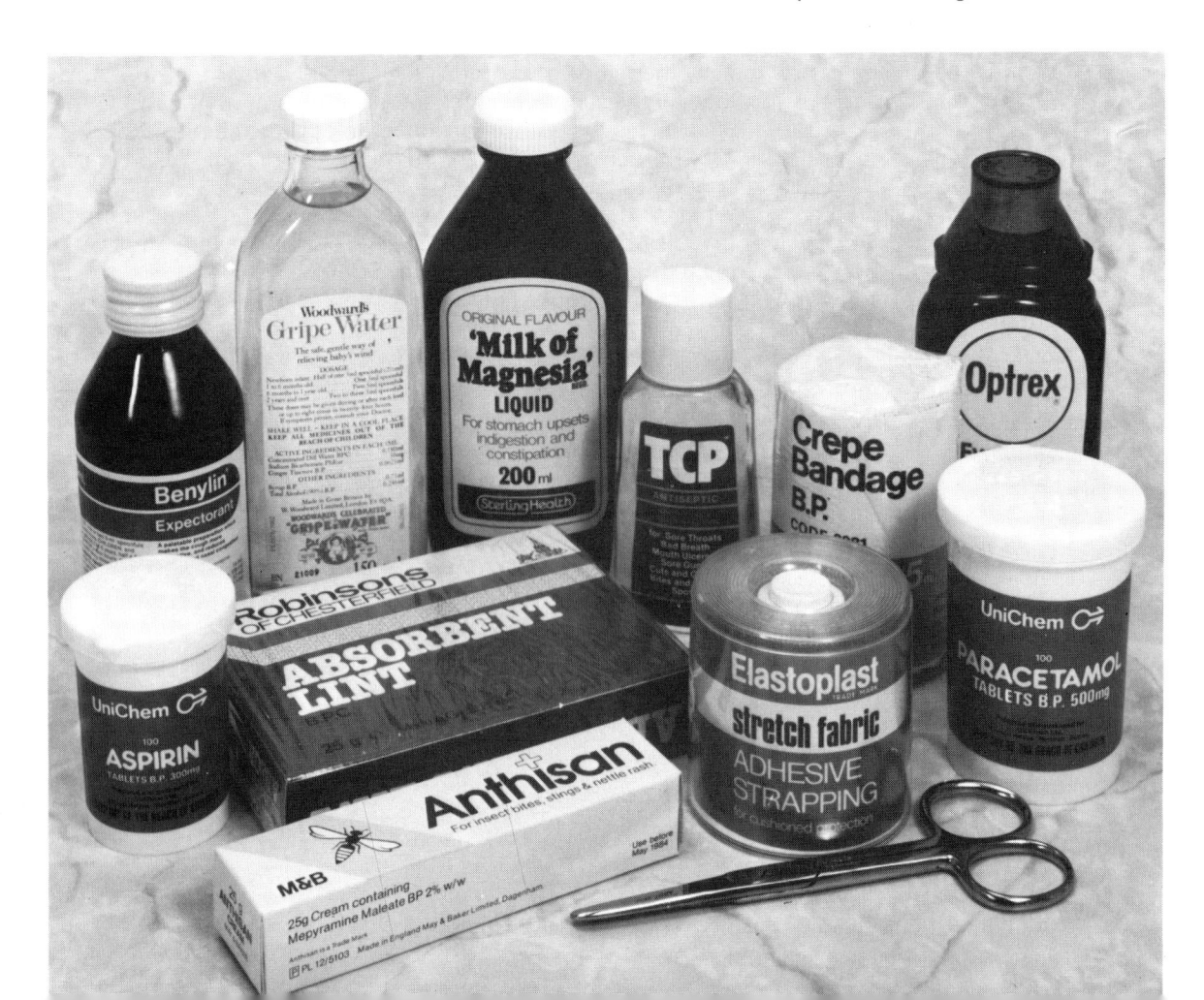

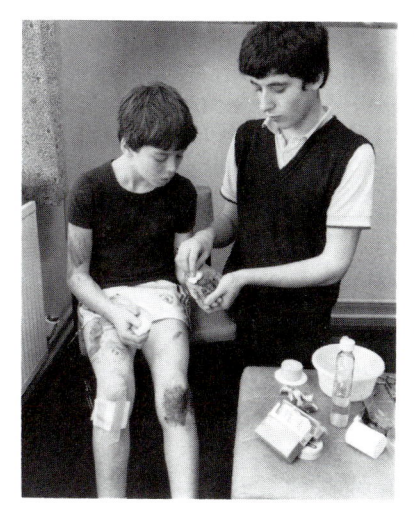

HOW TO KILL GERMS

Whatever you are doing with looking after someone who is unwell, you must guard against germs. Here is a list of ways of killing germs. Consult this list to answer the questions below:

boiling:	put the things to be cleaned in a clean saucepan, and boil them for several minutes. Make sure they are things that won't be damaged by boiling!
Milton:	a mild liquid disinfectant that kills germs but is harmless and almost free of taste if a little is swallowed when mixed with water.
Dettol, Ibcol etc.:	liquid disinfectants with a fairly strong smell.
TCP:	a strong germ killer. You can put a few drops on a cloth for cleaning the skin. Strong smell.
soap (not detergent) and hot water:	good at killing germs, but it needs to be washed off.
washing-up liquid:	removes grease but does not kill all the germs.
Jeyes' fluid, Jeypine etc.:	cheap strong disinfectants that must not be swallowed. Can be used by the bucketful if mixed with water.
open flame:	kills germs quickly but will damage many articles.

Which of the above would you use for cleaning:
a your hands
b a baby's bottle and teat
c a clinical thermometer
d wiping a graze
e wiping up vomit, when the dog has been sick all over the kitchen floor
f washing soiled clothes
g washing up plates, cups and cutlery from a person with a highly infectious germ
h cleaning a bagful of raw peaches that you dropped on the pavement
i treating a septic finger
j wiping off a table top that is known to have infectious germs on it?

KEEP THE PATIENT COMFY

a Patient has fainted, fallen unconscious, had an epileptic fit:
You should make sure the patient is in the recovery position, which means lying on his side, legs slightly pulled up, tight collar buttons or belts loosened, and kept warm with a coat. Doctor or ambulance may be needed, depending on what the cause is.

b Nosebleed:
The patient should sit quietly, with head slightly forward. Hold the top of the nose with gentle pressure. If it does not ease after a while, call the doctor.

c In bed with infection, migraine etc.:
Keep the patient   warm,
                   quiet,
                   in soft light,
                   with enough pillows

Offer light drinks –
                   squash and fruit juices,
                   weak tea, hot marmite, bovril, oxo, thin soup

Offer light food –
                   thin bread or toast
                   plain biscuits
                   small portions of thin lean meat

1 Look up as much as you can about the way to treat patients like these, and make notes of additional things you can do to make them comfortable.
2 What can you find out about the way to treat someone who might have a broken bone?
3 What is the correct treatment for someone who is choking on something he has swallowed?

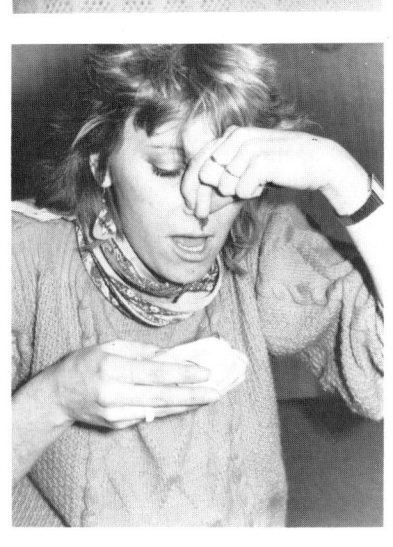

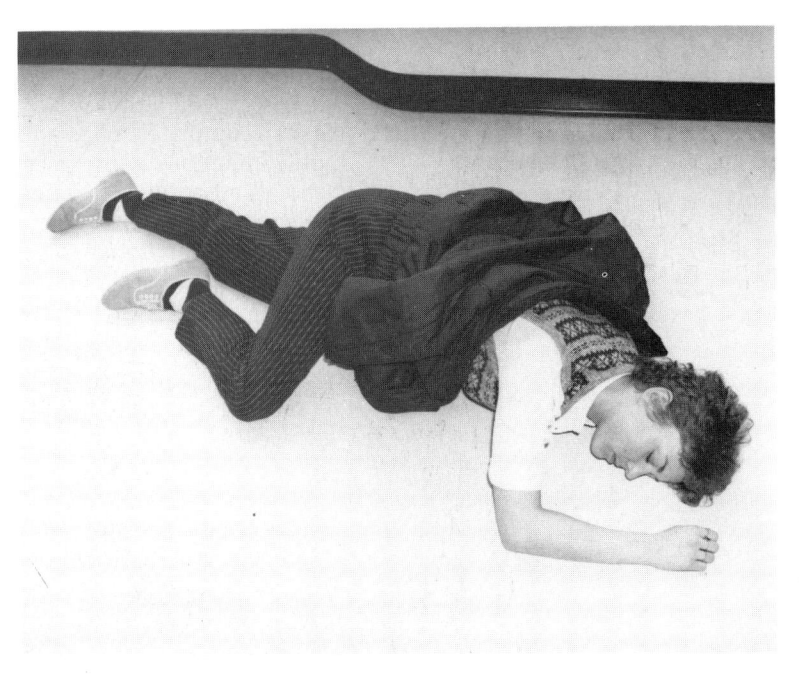

Tidying up your handwriting

Has anyone ever grumbled to you about your writing? Has anyone ever given you any idea how to make it better?

Here are some examples of writing by pupils in a comprehensive school. Let's see what's wrong with them.

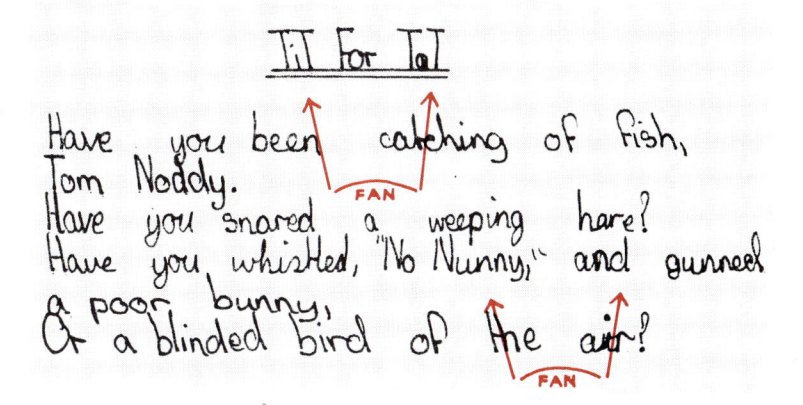

Can you see how this pupil has the stalks of all his letters sloping first one way and then the other way? Can you see how they make a fan? And how very untidy this makes his page? All he needs to do is to move his hand along the paper a little bit at the end of writing each word. Just now he has anchored his wrist and is stretching his fingers further and further along the line – and this is how he gets the fan effect. Good writing has all the stalks sloping the same way. It doesn't matter if it's backwards or forwards or straight up, so long as they are all the same.

Can you see how this girl's writing gets bigger and smaller in different places? Can you guess why? – Yes, she's sitting with her eyes so low down near the paper that when she is writing right up next to her nose even small letters seem big to her, but as she goes further along the line she has to write bigger just to keep it *looking* as if it's the same size. Cure – sit up straight with your eyes about 25 cms from the paper. You'll be able to see the whole page then, and keep the size even all the way along.

113

Bad pen grip. There is no control for shaping letters correctly.

The page may slip while you are writing. Steady it with your other hand.

Bad pen – messy page! You must have a good pen or a sharp pencil if you are to write well.

Not the way to sit. The lines won't be straight and the paper may slip.

The right way to sit and steady the paper.

A comfortable gentle pen grip which allows plenty of control.

Now try to do a bit of really good writing yourself. Copy something out so you don't have to think about what you're going to say next. Perhaps you'll choose a short poem, or a caption underneath a picture. Don't bother to do a lot; a hundred words is enough. And then score yourself on the checklist on the next page. Keep the piece you have written for looking at again later on.

Checklist

Have you got a good pen or a sharp pencil?
Are you sitting comfortably with good light?
Are your eyes about 25 cms from the paper, and your glasses on if you need them?
Are you holding the pen correctly?
Are you moving your hand along the line often enough?
Are you going the right way round each letter? See arrows on the chart opposite. (You start at the cross.)
Are your letters all the right size compared with each other? See chart.

Do the tails of your letters go below the line when they should?
See chart.
Do the stalks of your letters go above the line when they should?
See chart.
Are all your letters the right shape? Check the whole alphabet.
See chart.
Have you got capital letters mixed in where you should have small letters?

a b c d e f g h i
j k l m n o p q r
s t u v w x y z

A B C D E F G H I
J K L M N O P Q R
S T U V W X Y Z

a a a A o f t b d h k l g j p q y Z

If you're left handed –
Are you hiding your work as soon as you write it?
Can you position your hand up or down so that you can see what you have just written?

Did you make any mistakes in your piece of good writing? If you did, try writing it out again without these mistakes. It will need a bit of practice. Your mistakes have probably been going on for years and you are not going to put them right in a day.
Practise for a few minutes every day and then when you have got the hang of the right way, try to use it in all your work.
Compare your new tidy writing with that piece you analysed the first time.

Don't worry!
Lastly, here are some things NOT to worry about.

Don't worry about making your writing fit any particular style. Some people talk a lot about Italic, or Marion Richardson, or other styles, but very few people use them!

Don't worry about making all your letters join up. Join up some of them if you can – it's usually quicker – but very few people join them all up.

Don't worry if some people say your writing is too big or too small, so long as it is the same all the time. There are two questions to ask: (1) Can other people read it easily? (2) Do I like it myself? Your writing will say a lot about the sort of person you are, and that's how it should be.

TIME FOR ACTION!

1 Try writing these and other nonsense sentences, each of which have all the letters of the alphabet in them, and then swap your papers with your friends for detailed checking of the way you wrote each letter:
 a The film proved that the puzzling queen bee just licked the wax and honey we gave her.
 b In my quiz, six yellow jars had five green and black caterpillars.
 c Brian mixed the jelly we gave him while Liz quietly cut pieces of cake.
2 Some people say that you can tell that someone is a shy person or a bold person by the way they write. Do you think this is true about the way your friends write?
3 Which of these examples shown here do you like best, and why?

Trade unions

Over a period of many years, Unions have aimed to obtain better conditions for the workers. Discuss what changes are recorded on this page.

Bad luck mate – you're sacked.

You've not worked so hard this week, so I've cut your pay.

You've not finished yet. You don't expect to be paid until its all done, do you?

That's it. Closed down. No work, no pay.

- Conditions are different now. How big a part do you think the Unions have played in this?
- Have the Unions been successful in dealing with these and other issues?

Compensation £25,000.

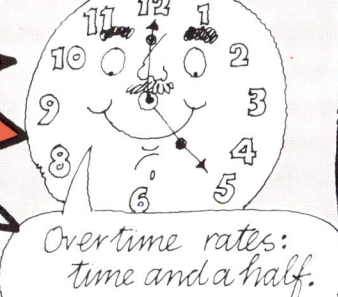

That's the rate per hour

De luxe WC

Overtime rates: time and a half.

Redundancy pay: £2480-00.

WHAT A UNION IS

A Union is a society of workers who have joined it because they do the same sort of work and they want to help each other make sure that the pay, conditions, and arrangements for their work are as good as they can be.

Even now, in the 1980s, in many countries it is against the law to belong to a Trade Union, and people may spend long periods in prison just because they joined one.

1. Will you be joining a Union when you leave school?
2. Do members of your family belong to Trade Unions?
3. Can you think of two or three reasons why other Governments would want to ban Unions?
4. Can you think of two or three things that would be much worse for many people in Britain if we did not have Unions?

The first Trade Unions were called Guilds. They were groups of workers who wanted to do three things. One was to protect their trade. Another was to make sure that young people could be trained in it. The third was to make sure that they would receive fair pay for the skill they used.

One sole worker who argues that he is overworked, underpaid, or made to work in unsafe or unhealthy conditions is not likely to win his argument. If the boss does not want to agree, he can wait till the worker leaves, and then take on another worker on the same conditions.

If workers agree to stand together, the boss who wants a job done has to take more notice. The job won't get done if all the workers stop working at the same time.

Some more points to discuss

1. The papers usually have news of a strike that is planned or happening somewhere in the country.
   From what you have heard about the reasons for one dispute going on just now, does it seem that the workers have a real problem? Have you sometimes thought that workers on strike were just being greedy?
2. The news makes it seem that there are always arguments in work places between 'the bosses' and 'the workers', but is this really true? Are there work places where everyone feels a member of a team, and such arguments do not often happen?
3. Working conditions in other countries are sometimes still as bad as they used to be in Britain. Do our Unions ever suggest anything that we can do about these other workers?

THE SKELETON STRUCTURE OF A UNION

This is an outline of how a large Union is organised:

1. The workers in a work place start talking together. They decide it is no good each one of them going to see the boss each time the heater fails, a safety guard falls off, or someone's pay is docked. They decide it would be best if one worker only went to speak for them all. So they vote for one, and he or she becomes their *shop steward*.

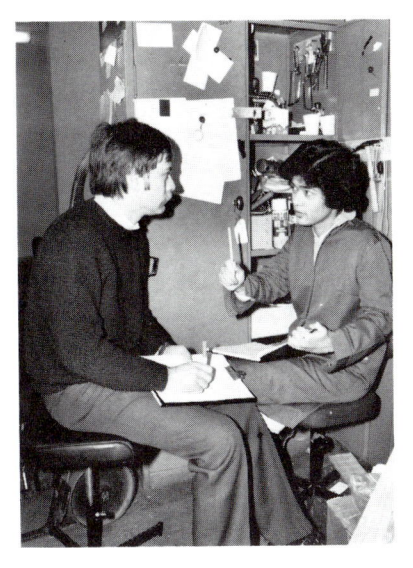

2. The shop steward goes on doing the same job for the same pay, but every time there is a problem he or she goes to see the boss. Usually the boss is quite helpful and the problem is soon sorted out. One day the boss does not agree with the shop steward, so the shop steward phones up the *branch secretary*.
3. The branch secretary used to be a shop steward but then he or she took some courses paid for by the Union in order to know more about the law and workers' rights, and now he or she is paid by the Union to help shop stewards when they have problems.
4. The branch secretary needs to know what the *Head Office* think about this particular problem, so he or she phones them up to ask.
5. The *Head Office* do not just give their own opinion. They look back at the record of what was said when chosen members (delegates) from all over the country last met together at an *Annual Conference*, because that was where they decided what would be best for all the members.

Choose one or two Unions that are strong locally, and give (a) the names of local workplaces where there are shop stewards (b) the address of the local branch secretary (c) the address of Head Office.

THE SMALLEST UNIONS IN THE T.U.C.

Some Unions are so small that each member must really feel he or she can be heard at the meetings.

Union	Number of members
Sawmakers' Protection Society, Sheffield	238
Military and Orchestra Musical Instrument Makers' Trade Society	226
Power Loom Over-Lookers (Scotland)	200
Healders and Twisters' Trade and Friendly Society, Huddersfield	174
Card Setting Machine Tenders' Society	130
The Society of Shuttlemakers	110
Pattern Weavers' Society	100
Spring Trapmakers' Society	90
Cloth Pressers' Society	30
Wool Shear Workers' Trade Union (Sheffield)	30

1. Which of these Unions are covering trades in the textile industry?
2. What reasons can you suggest why they may prefer to remain independent instead of joining with other larger Unions in the industry?
3. How would small Unions like these be able to protect the skilled interests of their members?

MEMBERSHIP OF TRADE UNIONS

Trade Group	No. of Unions	1976 Membership	1982 Membership
Mining and Quarrying	3	276 636	289 448
Railways	3	272 762	277 051
Other Forms of Transport	6	1 966 303	2 203 515
Shipbuilding	1	129 598	129 712
Engineering, Founding, and Vehicle Building	10	1 499 511	1 449 800
Technical Engineering and Scientific	3	523 242	745 063
Electricity	1	414 189	420 000
Iron and Steel and Minor Metal Trades	9	144 473	137 998
Building, Woodworking and Furnishing	3	346 830	435 493
Printing and Paper	5	306 582	429 257
Textiles	13	130 092	111 886
Clothing, Leather and Boot and Shoe	6	262 553	259 561
Glass, Ceramics, Chemicals, Food, Drink, Tobacco, Brushmaking and Distribution	9	495 506	606 018
Agriculture	1	90 000	85 000
Public Employees	12	1 615 452	2 235 985
Civil Servants and Post Office	13	785 696	959 116
Professional, Clerical and Entertainment	10	270 489	430 452
General Workers	1	883 810	967 153
	109	10 363 724	12 172 508

1. Which trade group is now the largest employment group in the country?
2. Which trade group is now the second largest employment group in the country?
3. How many Unions altogether serve these two groups of workers?
4. Which trade group has had a growth of 620 533 Union members in the five year period?
5. Which trade group has had a growth of 221 821 Union Members during the five year period?
6. Which four trade groups have had a reduction in the number of Union members during the five year period?
7. Can you suggest reasons why there have been these changes in numbers of workers in the different groups?
8. Which trade groups are most unlikely to have many members in your home region? How many workers do they have in the country as a whole?

THE LARGEST TRADE UNIONS

The names of the Trade Unions that have more than 250 000 members each, and their membership figures in 1982, are:

Transport and General Workers' Union	2 086 281
Amalgamated Union of Engineering Workers	1 217 760
National Union of General and Municipal Workers	967 153
National and Local Government Officers' Association	753 226
National Union of Public Employees	691 770
Association of Scientific, Technical and Managerial Staffs	491 000
Union of Shop, Distributive, and Allied Workers	470 017
Electrical, Electronic, Telecommunications and Plumbing Union	420 000
Union of Construction, Allied Trades and Technicians	347 777
National Union of Mineworkers	253 142

1 Explain the meanings of these words which are used in the names of the Unions:
 (a) Amalgamated (b) Municipal (c) Officers
 (d) Managerial.
2 What is the difference in meaning between the words in these pairs? (a) Technical and Technicians (b) Electrical and Electronic
3 If each branch of the Transport and General Workers' Union had a thousand members, how many branches would there be?
4 If each branch of the National Union of Mineworkers had five hundred members, how many branches would there be?
5 What are the full names of the Unions which are often simply called 'Nalgo', 'Nupe', 'Usdaw', 'Aslef', and 'Natsopa'?
6 Ask people you know who belong to any of these Unions for recent copies of campaign leaflets. Discuss together what the members are worried about just now.

UNION WORDS

Here are some important Union words, and some explanations of what they mean. Match the words to the meanings.

shop steward	T.U.C.	branch secretary	arbitration
official strike	closed shop	unofficial strike	lock out
delegate	blackleg	national conference	redundancy pay

- a worker chosen by other workers in one part of a factory or work place to speak for them. An unpaid official, who still does his ordinary work in the factory.
- all the workers refusing to do any more work until their demands are met, with the backing of their Union.
- workers refusing to do any more work until their demands are met, without the backing of their Union.
- full time official, paid from members' subscriptions; he no longer does his ordinary job in the factory, so as to have time for Union work.

121

- Union member chosen to go to a conference.
- meeting of delegates from every Union, in which common problems or ideas are discussed.
- calling in an outsider to settle an argument, usually between Unions and employers.
- a rule that says that everyone who does a particular job must be a member of a particular Union.
- money that is paid to you if your employer does not want your job done any more.
- when the people who run a factory (etc.) refuse to allow workers to do their work.
- someone who goes to work when the rest of the Union are on strike.

WOMEN IN THE UNIONS

There are not as many women workers in the Unions as there are men. The Unions with most women members are:

T.& G.W.U.   N.A.L.G.O.
N.U.G.& M.W.   N.U.P.E.
U.S.D.A.W.

1. Can you suggest two or three reasons why there are not as many women in Unions?
2. What are the full names of the Unions that do have a lot of women members?
3. What sort of jobs are many of the women members likely to be doing?
4. Why would many women be willing to do a job and yet not be particularly keen to join a Union?
5. What differences can it make to all the other workers if a lot of people are willing to work without joining a Union?

Issues to discuss

There are many issues to worry both the workers and the management, that Union members need to think about. What opinions do you have on these?

1. Would you ever think of going to work across a picket line? Give your reasons.
2. Is it fair to make 'closed shops' and say that people cannot have a particular job until they join the Union?
3. What do you think a Union member should say if new machines are brought in that make some workers redundant, but the management insist either costs are cut or they close down completely?
4. What news have you heard about Unions helping the unemployed, or are they only helping those who have got jobs?
5. Does the T.U.C. seem to have helped the Unions to decide together about pay rises and their attitudes to redundancy, unemployment, and holidays, or do one or two Unions seem to be trying to get more than the other Unions this year?
6. Do you know anyone who has been on strike in the past year? If so, can you find out (a) what problems were met (b) if the person thinks the strike was necessary.

Using banks and cheques

Discuss together which of these 'money shops' is the most useful place to keep an account:

- National Savings Bank
- Post Office Giro
- Ordinary Banks (Lloyds, Midland, Barclays, National Westminster etc)
- Trustee Savings Banks
- Building Societies
- Other banks, like the Co-operative Bank or People's Bank

You will have to find out some things about each of these before you can decide which is best. Visit some of them and ask for details. Go to the Post Office for the forms about the Savings Bank and Giro. Then draw out a grid like this and fill in what you can find out about each place for keeping your money:

Question	National Savings Bank	P.O. Giro	Ordinary Bank (Big Four)	Trustee Savings Bank	Building Society	Other Bank (which?)
Do you get interest on your account? How much?						
How much cash can you get on demand? How long do you have to wait to get more than this?						
How many places can you go to to get your money out? (branches) How long are they open?						
Can you put in as much money as you like?						
Can you use cheques on this account?						
When you are 18, and they know you, will you be able to have credit cards or overdraw this account?						
Will you have to pay tax on the interest if you earn enough?						
What other services are provided with this account?						

AT THE POST OFFICE

Two forms of account are run at the Post Office – the National Savings Bank and the Giro. Besides this, there are many certificates and bonds that you can buy as a way of investing your money, but these are not accounts – you cannot keep putting money in and taking it out again.

Here are examples of the forms that you need to put money in and take money out of the National Savings Bank. Check that you can fill the forms in correctly by putting down on a piece of paper all the entries you should make on these forms if you carried out these transactions:

Use your own name and address with the postal code.
The account is opened on the 3rd of this month.
Your account number is 234-567-890.
You start by depositing £25.00.
Then on the 10th of this month you deposit another £12.50.
And on the 17th of this month another £7.50.
Your fourth transaction is on the 3rd of next month, when you deposit £35.00.
Then on the 5th of next month you have to withdraw £18.00.
Remember, a signature is not just writing your name. If you haven't yet developed a signature of your own, begin some experiments now. It is a good idea to include the initials of your middle names, and you may (or may not) like to write your first name in full. Try to get a signature that looks much the same every time you write it.

Then on the 29th of next month you deposit a further £32.00.

And on the 13th of the month after next you withdraw £30.00.

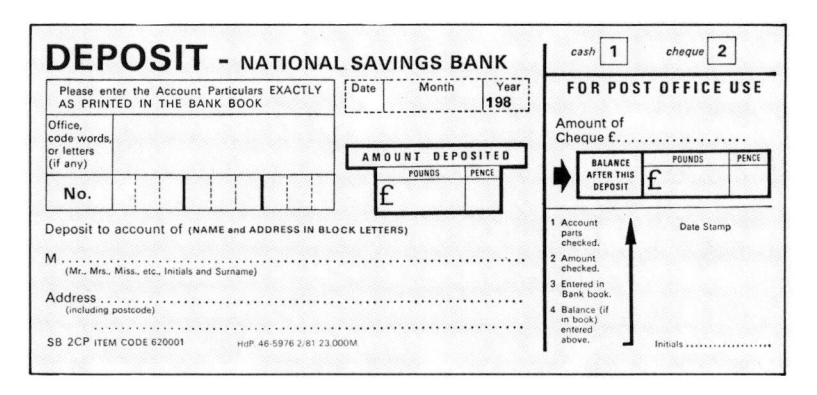

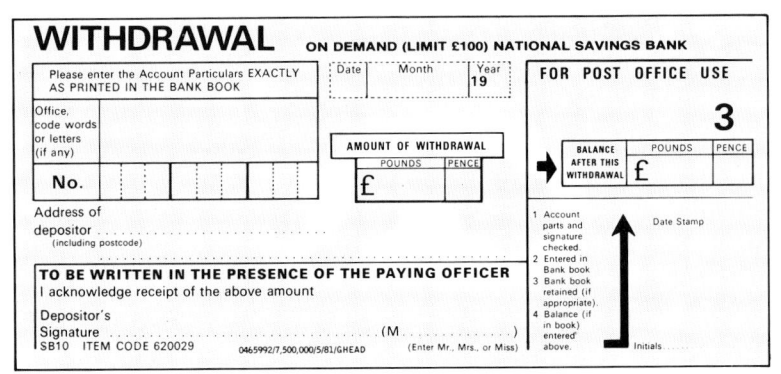

Finally, try your hand at a Giro Inpayment. For the Giro account number, use 64 653 2179. Use the Giro form to pay £15.55 to Trendy Fashions P.L.C., and fill in your own name and address as 'payer'.

USING CHEQUES

A cheque is a piece of paper that a bank gives you to fill in when you want to pay someone else. If it is crossed it has two lines drawn across it, as you can see on the one shown here. A crossed cheque has to be paid into a bank account before the other person can have the money. If it has not got the lines on it, it is called an open cheque, and it is possible to take it to a bank and exchange it for cash. So if someone drops an open cheque there is more chance that a dishonest person might use it to collect the money. Crossed cheques are safer.

Cheques are usually supplied in cheque books, and you tear the cheque off from the stub each time you make a payment. Most people like to keep a record on the stub of what they have just paid out, and many people do a quick take-away sum there. They put down the amount they know they had in the account, and take away the amount of the cheque, so they find out how much is left in the account for any more cheques they may write.

Once a bank knows you well enough they may allow you to overdraw, which means to spend a little bit more than you actually have in the account at that time, but the manager will want to see you and will ask questions to find out why you really need to borrow money in this way. It is illegal to borrow money until you are 18. If you were to write a cheque for more than you have at the time, without the bank's permission, the cheque will 'bounce', which means that the bank will refuse to pay out the money.

Banks issue Credit Cards and Banker's Cards to customers over 18 who have kept good accounts with them. Many shops insist on seeing one of these before they will agree to accept a cheque. The card proves to the shop that they will get the money you are paying.

When you are writing out a cheque remember
- the correct date
- the name of the person you want to pay
- how much you want to pay, written out in words
- how much you want to pay, written out in numbers
- your signature
- cross it if you want to, and if it has not already been printed as a crossed cheque.

1. How do you know if a cheque has been crossed?
2. What can go wrong with an open cheque?
3. What use are Bankers' Cards?
4. What is a cheque stub for?
5. How old must you be to borrow money?
6. What does to 'overdraw' an account mean?
7. What does it mean if a cheque 'bounces'?
8. What limit is there to how much you can pay on one cheque?

Try your hand at writing some cheques. If you can have a supply of 'imitation cheques', write out cheques for the payment of all the bills in the accounts shown on the next page.

THE ACCOUNT SHEET

Whatever sort of bank account you have, you will want to be able to make sense of the statement of account that they send you, to make sure that they have kept the record right.

Most statements include the information that is shown opposite, although the order in which the columns come, and the letters that are used for the different sorts of credit and debit, will not be the same in each bank.

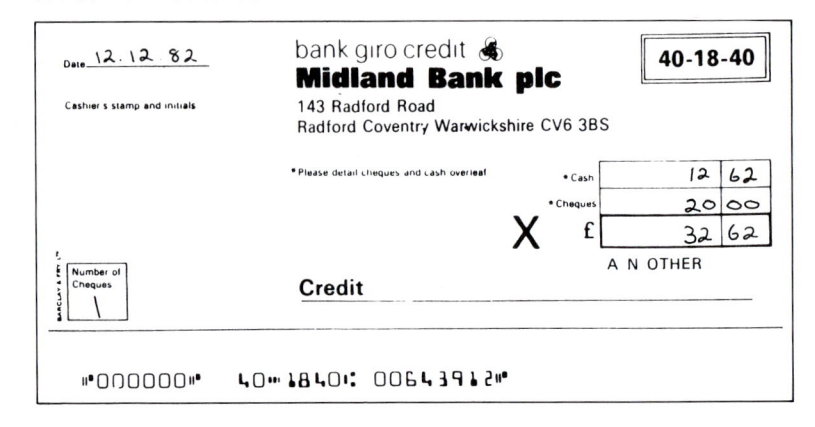

A credit is a record of money put in, to increase the amount you have in the account, which is called the balance. A debit is a record of money taken out, and this reduces the amount you have left in the account (the balance). Complete your own record of account for these two customers, working out the balance as you do so.

Use the same headings as in the example here.

Detail	Payments (Debit)	Receipts (Credit)	Date	Balance

Tom Midas

31 March	Receive pay	£468.32
3 April	Pay Building Society	£158.48
7 April	Pay Life Assurance	£23.30
8 April	Pay District Council	£174.38
8 April	Draw cash	£50.00
12 April	Pay Autocross P.L.C.	£27.50
17 April	Draw cash	£50.00
23 April	Pay Gas Board	£34.15

Tanya Gold

27 May	Receive pay	£399.99
5 June	Pay Building Society	£164.39
10 June	Pay Eastern Electricity Board	£89.13
3 June	Draw cash	£100.00
14 June	Pay Debenham's P.L.C.	£13.99
23 June	Pay Mail Order Catalogues P.L.C.	£23.45
4 July	Pay L. Turner	£29.03

```
     A N OTHER ESQ                              40-18-40
     14 LONG STREET                                ---001
     COVENTRY                                    B000001
     WARWICKSHIRE                                  B0001
     CV6 4OS


A N OTHER                    Midland Bank plc
                             143 RADFORD ROAD RADFORD
                             COVENTRY WARWICKS CV6 38S

                             Statement of Account

                             DEBIT        CREDIT            BALANCE
1982    Sheet 001  Account No. 00643912                  Credit C  Debit D
NOV  5  CREDIT TRANSFER                    21.55          21.55 C
NOV  8  100231               15.00                         6.55 C
NOV 10  STANDING ORDER        2.56                         3.99 C
NOV 12  CREDIT TRANSFER                    21.26          25.25 C
NOV 16  100233               12.00                        13.25 C
NOV 16  100232                7.00                         6.25 C
NOV 17  STANDING ORDER        2.56                         3.69 C
NOV 19  CREDIT TRANSFER                    30.64          34.33 C
NOV 23  100234               10.00                        24.33 C
NOV 25  STANDING ORDER        2.56                        21.77 C
NOV 26  CREDIT TRANSFER                    25.96          47.73 C
NOV 30  100235               15.00                        32.73 C
DEC  2  STANDING ORDER        2.56                        30.17 C
DEC  3  CREDIT TRANSFER                    21.55          51.72 C
DEC  6  BALANCE CARRIED FORWARD                           51.72 C
```

Using a calculator

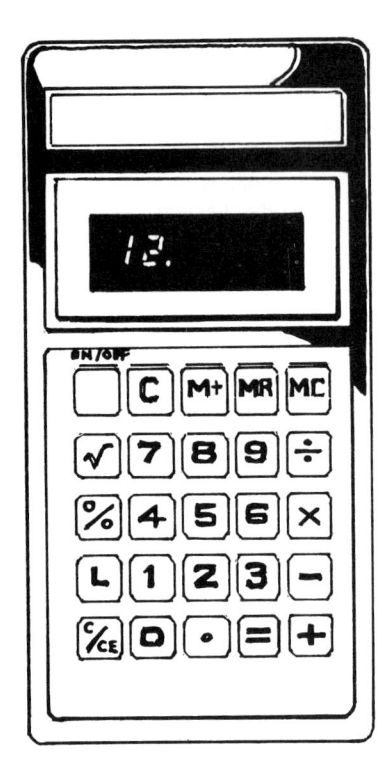

It's easy enough to use a calculator.
It's not so easy to get every answer right!
One good rule is:
always check every sum twice and make sure you get the same answer each time.
That helps to cut down mistakes that come from hitting the wrong keys, or not pressing hard enough, or accidentally pressing twice.

One useful key on most calculators is CE. This means you can rub out just the last figures you have put in since the last "function" sign (+, −, ÷, ×). It saves going right back to the beginning of the sum.

Remember with sums that when you see the words 'out of' it usually means ÷, and when you see 'of' it means ×. 'From' means −, and 'and' means +.
Be careful to key the figures in in the right order.

Can you be sure to get the right answers to these sums?

1. 1 000 × 1 000 + 111 111 − 999 999 − 1 ÷ 3
2. 8% of 13 325
3. 2.5% of 77 800
4. 12 345 678 ÷ 18 − 1 × 0.5 − 9 602
5. 45% of £90.00

And these? (Work to the nearest penny.)

6. Diane had a pay rise of 8.75% of £45.72
7. David had a pay rise of 7.93% of £50.45
8. Daphne did a survey of 3 924 people and found that 1 962 of them drank white coffee. How many did not drink white' coffee?
9. Dimitri did a survey of 1 066 people and found that 511 of them had a musical instrument at home. How many did not?
10. Delia checked her week's expenses. She had spent £13.82 in Sainsbury's, £15.00 in British Home Stores, £8.36 in Halford's, £3.99 in Mothercare, £14.50 in the Co-op, £7.99 in Marks and Spencer, £3.25 in Littlewood's, 75p in Woolworth's, £8.88 in Debenham's, and £2.47 in Boots. How much had she left from the £100.00 she had had at the start of the week?

USING THE CALCULATOR MEMORY

The Memory key can be very useful. Many sums have two stages. You can either write down the answer to the first stage on a piece of paper, or you can put it in memory (M+). When you want to bring it back in to your working you press MR (Memory Recall). When you don't need it stored any more you press MC (Memory Clear).

For example, you might want to add up the cost of the shopping, such as:
£17.99 and £12.47 and two items at £7.60 each with 10% discount and £25.45. The right way to do this is:

17.99	+	12.47	M+	C	7.60	×	10
%	−	=	×	2	+	MR	+	25.45	=
MC	C

Or to take a simpler example, you might want to add $\frac{1}{4} + \frac{2}{3}$

So you press | 1 | ÷ | 4 | and then | M+ |, and clear the display | C |. Then you do | 2 | ÷ | 3 | and bring in the other part | + | MR | and press | = | to find the answer, which is given as a decimal and not a 'vulgar' fraction. (Then clear the Memory | MC | and the display | C |).

If you are doing a take-away sum you must make sure you do things in the right order. If you are asked what is one less than two you don't say $1 - 2 = -1$, but $2 - 1 = 1$, and the same is the case on the calculator:

What is $\frac{1}{4}$ less than $\frac{2}{3}$? goes:

| 2 | ÷ | 3 | M+ | C | 1 | ÷ | 4 | − | MR | = |
| MC | C |

Can you get the right answers to these sums, using Memory in each case? The order is shown for you on some; the others follow the same pattern.

| 3 | ÷ | 4 | M+ | C | 2 | ÷ | 3 | + | MR | = | | MC | C |

1. $\frac{3}{4} + \frac{2}{3}$
2. $\frac{14}{15} + \frac{11}{12}$
3. $\frac{14}{15} - \frac{7}{12}$
4. £13.45 + £22.50 + two items at 14% less than £5.50
5. £6.94 + £16.87 + three items at 12% less than £12.50
6. One in four of 1 296 pupils in Barkley School have dogs
   | 1 | ÷ | 4 | × | 1 296 |
   and one in three of all the pupils have cats.
   | + | 1 | ÷ | 3 | × | 1 296 |
   How many have one or both as pets?
7. Three quarters of the 1 296 pupils in Barkley School have a pet of some kind, but only one in twelve of the ones with pets have more than three pets. How many have more than three pets?
8. One in seven of the 1 008 pupils at Warrenthwaite School have a rabbit, but only one in nine of the rabbit owners has a big garden. How many pupils have a rabbit in a big garden?
9. Seven out of eight of the 952 pupils at Llancorn School have a pet of some sort, but only three in every seven pupils use their own pocket money to buy food for it. How many use their own pocket money to buy food?
10. Eleven out of twelve of the 792 pupils at Inverpark School had already visited a zoo once, and six out of every eleven of them all had been twice. How many zoo tickets had they bought altogether?

Using a dictionary

No one made up the English language. Nearly every word has come in from some other language. English is a very rich language because it has words from so many languages in it. It is living, growing and changing. New meanings come for old words.

The *Oxford English Dictionary* has a short note about every word in our language. There are so many words in the language that no other dictionary can put them all in.

But in day by day use we do not need a dictionary with so many words. There are a lot of smaller dictionaries to choose from in the shops.

WHAT ARE DICTIONARIES FOR?

Most dictionaries tell us at least five things about a word:
- What it means
- How to spell it
- How to say it
- How to use it
- What language the word came from.

Modern dictionaries often include some general information. Special dictionaries are used to translate from one language to another.

READING A DICTIONARY

It's not easy to read a dictionary. Many words are cut short to save space. The most important of these shortenings are:

a.
adj. } = adjective

n. = noun

v.
v.i. } = verb
v.t.

~ = repeat the word already printed in heavy type

There are other shortenings that are used in almost every dictionary. These are:
 etc = et cetera (and so on)
 adv. = adverb
 prep. = preposition

WHAT DOES IT MATTER IF A WORD IS A NOUN?

Many words can be used in more than one way.
A *noun* is a word that *names* a thing, place, or person. For example, a coconut *shy* (n.) can be found at a fair.
A *verb* is a word that tells us about *doing* something. For example, a horse will *shy* (v.) when it is frightened.
An *adjective* is a word that tells us what something is *like*, for example, some people are *shy* (adj.).
To find the right meaning you must make sure that you are looking up the word being used the right way.

Look at the dots and spots
It is very important to look carefully at the punctuation marks. They have all been put there with a job to do.

● Often a word can mean something that is not quite the same as any other word, but a little bit in between. The dictionary will write these down with a comma in between, like this:

ragged: Rough, shaggy, hanging down in tufts.

● Many words have more than one meaning. These different meanings are separated with a semi-colon, like this:

rugged: Of rough, uneven surface; lacking gentleness or refinement.

● Hints to the right way to say the word may be given in brackets, straight after the word itself, if the spelling is not clear, like this:

ragged (-g-)	The tramp had ragged clothes.
rigged (-gd)	He rigged up a contraption.
rigid	There were rigid rules in the school.
rugged (-g-)	A man with a rugged face.

● Sometimes there are quite different words that are all spelt the same. These will be numbered in a dictionary, like this:

rail[1] n.	Iron bar.
rail[2] n.	Kind of bird. Water ~
rail[3] v.i.	Use abusive language.

Some words have meanings that are so different that they are not separated with a semi-colon, but each meaning is given a number. Look at the pictures and see how many meanings of the word "point" you can write down. There are other meanings of the word that you cannot show in a picture. Have you got the point?

1 How many different meanings are given in the dictionary for these words:
   a line   d box
   b bow   e form
   c play   f light

2 Dots and spots also help you to know which bit of a word to give most stress to. When we speak English we usually put most of the stress on one part of a word and let the other parts be said quietly. The dictionary marks the part of the word that has the stress with a mark like this after it: '.

   Where do we put the stress on these words?
   a social   g hypochondria
   b sociable   h invalid = sick
   c society   i invalid = not valid
   d hypocaust   j peculiarity
   e hypocrisy   k thoroughfare
   f hypodermic   l representative

NOW CAN YOU USE A DICTIONARY?

3 Here are some words that are used a lot by employers. Can you say them all, and do you know what they all mean?
   a personnel   f industrious
   b confidentiality g integrity
   c responsibility   h conscientiousness
   d persistence   i punctuality
   e motivation   j perseverance

Visiting work places

A WASTE OF TIME

A visit to a work place can be a waste of time
- if you can't hear what the guide says,
- if you don't try to find out about it,
- if you don't look around to see what there is and what is going on,
- if you don't bother to think about what it would be like to work there.

Why do these things matter on a visit?
a What shoes you wear
b How hungry you feel
c Passing on what the guide says to those at the back of the group
d Listening to safety regulations
e Saying 'thank you'
f Not touching stock or machines.

A CUSHY NUMBER?

Conditions at work vary enormously: sewage farm workers expect different conditions to the private secretary of the Managing Director of a prosperous firm. What sort of work place would have these features, and why? Would you like to work in these conditions and surroundings?

Thick colourful carpets
Good strip lighting and background music
Bare concrete floors
Comfortable, carpeted, relaxation areas
Pin-ups of nude girls
Ear mufflers or dark glasses
Nowhere to sit down
Indoor plants for decoration

KEEP YOUR EYES OPEN!

Even if you can't hear what the guide says, there is a lot you can find out. Make your own list of questions that you could answer just by looking. They can include how many different types of job you see (e.g. receptionist, van driver), age range of employees met, how hard people were working, variety of work done by each person, types of machine available, comfort, end products.

Voting-for what?

When you are 18 you can vote.
You can vote for your local council and for your M.P. and your M.E.P.
How will you decide how to vote?
What difference does it make anyway?

Your vote is counted in an area. If you are voting for the British Parliament the area is quite big and is called a Constituency. If you are voting for the Council the area is much smaller and is called a Ward. If you are voting for the European Parliament the area is a very big Constituency.

For years, British voting rules have said that the winner is the person with most votes. If there are more than two people standing, the one with the highest number of votes wins, even if he or she has less than half the total votes. Your vote might make all the difference!

PROPORTIONAL REPRESENTATION

In many other countries they add up the votes for each party in a block of, say, six constituencies or wards, and share out the places. Each party has a list of candidates. The candidate at the top of the list is the most likely one to win a seat, and the one at the bottom of the list would only win a seat if the party got most of the votes. This system is called Proportional Representation.

Work out what the results of these elections would be on
(a) the traditional British system   (b) Proportional Representation

Constituency	GENERAL Conservative	ELECTION Labour	RESULTS Liberal and Social Democratic Party Alliance	Others	Total Votes
A	30 000	13 000	25 000	500	68 500
B	30 000	8 000	15 000	1 500	54 500
C	20 000	21 000	15 000	2 000	58 000
D	5 000	20 000	15 000	500	40 500
E	8 000	25 000	15 000	4 000	52 000
F	22 000	8 000	20 000	500	50 500

Total votes per party (add up votes for each party) divided by average number of votes per seat (54 000) = number of seats on Proportional Representation

324 000 divided by the total number of constituencies (6) = an average 54 000 votes per seat

1 How many seats were won by the Conservatives on the traditional system?
2 How many seats were won by the Conservatives on Proportional Representation?

3 How many seats were won by the Alliance on the traditional system?
4 How many seats were won by the Alliance on Proportional Representation?
5 Only in one seat did a party win more than half the votes. Which result was it?
6 Which candidate for the 'others' should be given a seat?

NATIONAL GOVERNMENT

1 Which party is in power just now?
2 Who is the Prime Minister?
3 Who is Chancellor of the Exchequer?
4 Who is the Leader of the Opposition?
5 Which party does your local M.P. belong to?

HOW THE GOVERNMENT MAY AFFECT YOU

- You pay your tax to the Inland Revenue (including V.A.T.)
- You claim your Sickness Benefit from the Department of Health and Social Security.
- You claim Supplementary and Unemployment Benefit from the Department of Health and Social Security.
- The Department of Education and Science fixes the School Leaving Age.

Most Governments have about twenty Ministries and Departments. Here are the names of six that may come to your notice. Can you find out what the others are?

- Inland Revenue, controlled by the Chancellor of the Exchequer, collects all the taxes from you – V.A.T. as well as Income Tax.
- Department of Trade and Industry, including the actions of the Minister of Trade on such matters as shop hours, packaging, and monopolies.
- Department of Health and Social Security, including the actions of the Minister of Health on such matters as sickness benefit, prescription charges and money provided for hospitals.
- Department of Education and Science, including the actions of the Under Secretary of State for Schools about examinations, and money available for schools.
- Department of the Environment, including the actions of the Minister of Transport on such matters as regulations for vehicles or driving licences.

NATIONAL POLITICAL PARTIES

The biggest political parties found in all parts of Britain are:
  The Labour Party (with the Co-operative Party)
  The Conservative Party
  The Liberal Party
  The Social Democratic Party (S.D.P.)

Parties with strong support in some parts of the country are the Scottish Nationalists, The Welsh Nationalists (Plaid Cymru), and local parties in Northern Ireland. A number of other parties contest some seats.

POLICIES OF THE BIG POLITICAL PARTIES (PART ONE)

The differences between the national parties may become clear if you can find out the answers to fill in a copy of this table. Try to decide if the policy of the party means 'more', 'less' or the 'same' for each box.

Subject	Conservative	Labour	Liberal	Social Democrats	One Other If You Wish
Reducing Income Tax most for low-paid					
How high V.A.T. should be					
Taxing rich people more					
Increasing pensions					
Supporting pay rises for low paid workers					
Allowing big pay rises for managers					
Extending state control (nationalisation)					

To find the policies of the parties, you can write to their district branches for the latest manifesto. The addresses will be in the telephone book.

POLICIES OF THE BIG POLITICAL PARTIES (PART TWO)

Collect information in the same way to complete this table. Try to decide if the policy of the party means they are 'keen', 'not keen', or want 'no change'.

Subject	Conservative	Labour	Liberal	Social Democrats	One Other If You Wish
Keeping private health service					
Leaving E.E.C.					
Updating nuclear weapons					
Building nuclear power stations					
Voting by proportional representation					
Helping people buy their own homes					
Building more council houses					
Encouraging private schools					
Paying big grants to students					
Paying good grants to those in great need (e.g. one-parent families).					

Words to do with politics

There are a lot of special words to do with politics.
Read through this list carefully.
Then work in pairs: your partner reads out what the word means and you try to say which word it is.
Take it in turns. Can you score more than your partner?

Bill:
a plan for a new law to be discussed by Parliament.

Manifesto:
what a party says it will do if elected.

White Paper:
a suggestion for a new law that could be made into a Bill later.

Act:
a new law which has been passed by Parliament.

House of Commons:
where all the M.P.s meet to discuss new laws.

Candidate:
someone who wants to be elected.

Cabinet:
the most important members of the government – usually about 20 people.

Left wing:
people who belong to the Labour Party or have similar views.

Party:
a group of people who have the same ideas and want to win elections so as to carry out these ideas.

Electoral register.
list of everyone allowed to vote.

Prime Minister:
the person who is in charge of the Government, appointed by the Queen after winning an election.

Right wing:
people who belong to the Conservative Party or have similar views.

Chancellor of the Exchequer:
the person who is in charge of the country's money, appointed by the Prime Minister.

Government:
the Prime Minister and the other Ministers he or she appoints – altogether about 100; the Civil Service helps them to carry out their policies.

Civil Service:
about ½ million people paid to administer the government of the country.

By-election:
an election for one particular seat (on the local council or in Parliament) held on a different date from the main election.

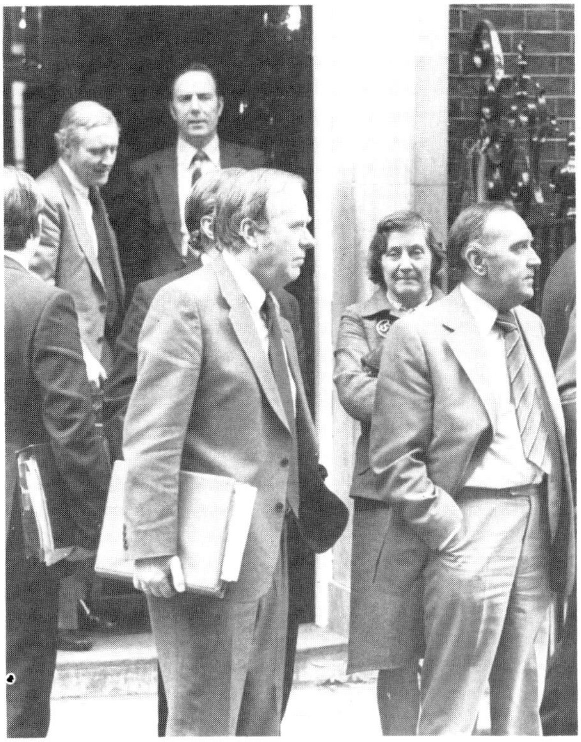

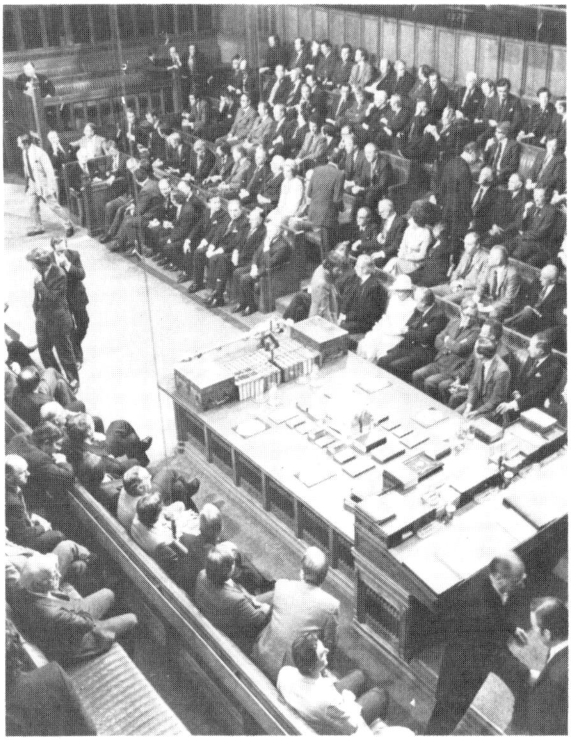

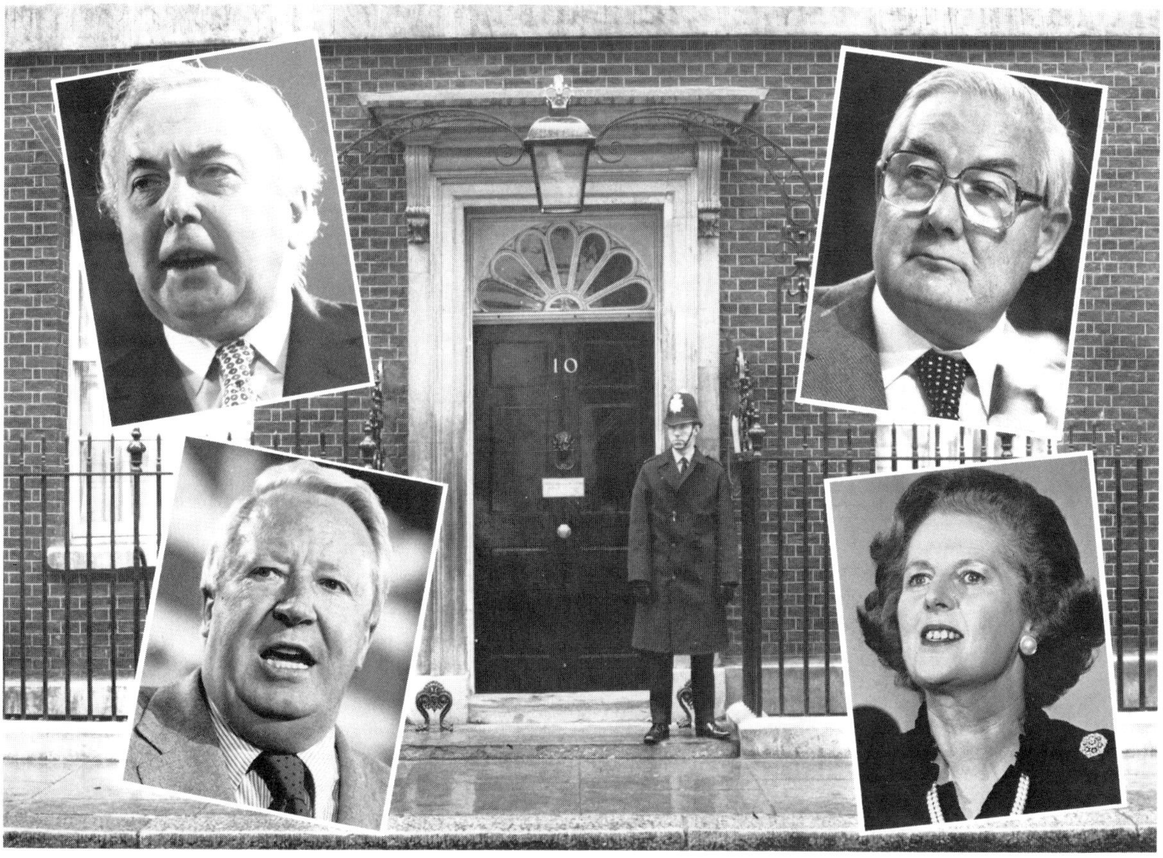
10

YOUR LOCAL COUNCIL

The country is divided into counties (see page 22), and each county has a County Council. The members of this Council are elected by the people who live in the county. Besides this, each county is split into districts, and the districts have Councils. The people who live in the district elect their District Councillors. London is divided into boroughs (see page 27), and other densely populated areas into Metropolitan District Councils. Scotland has Regional Councils instead of County Councils.

The people who are elected as councillors are in charge of all the arrangements for some aspects of life in the district or the county. They decide how much local tax to charge people (this is called the rates), and the Government also send them some of the tax collected by the Inland Revenue. The councillors appoint full-time permanent staff who work at County Hall or in the council offices, and each department usually has a large workforce. This chart shows part of this system. Can you complete the missing parts?

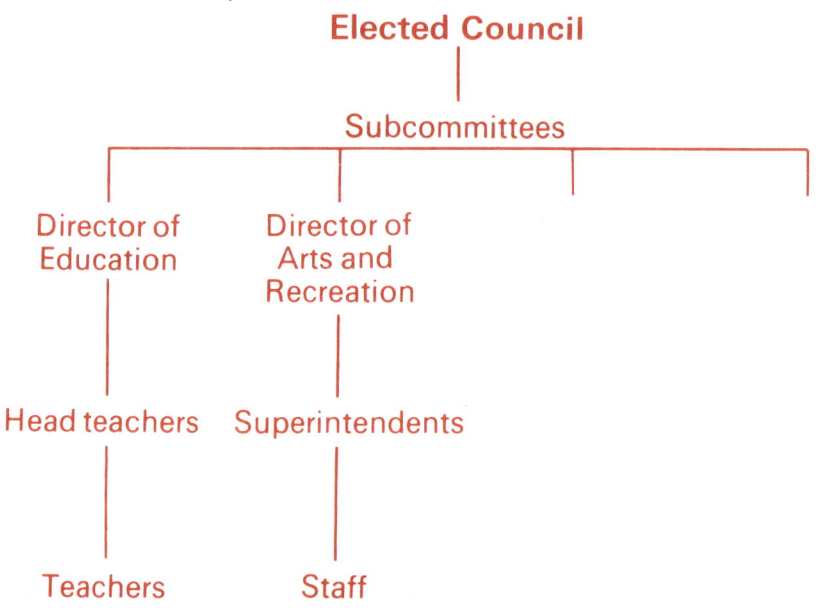

Elected Council
|
Subcommittees
┌──────────┬──────────┬──────────┐
Director of   Director of
Education   Arts and
                Recreation
| |
Head teachers   Superintendents
| |
Teachers   Staff

1. What staffing is concerned with aspects of transport? For example, your local council is concerned with local roads. The Government Department of the Environment deals with Motorways, and the County Council deals with roads that are classified as 'A' and 'B' roads.
2. The Council looks after libraries and museums. How many of these are in your district? What staff are employed?
3. The Council is responsible for social services in the district, including children's homes, social workers, and old people's homes. What staff are involved on these activities?
4. Which party is in control of your local Council at the present time, and is this the same party that it has been in recent years? Have there been any big changes of policy in recent years?

The weather forecast

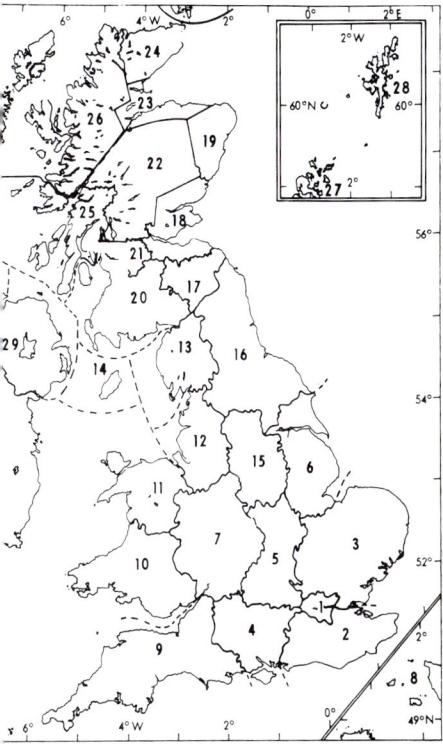

Do you manage to make the best use of a weather forecast? Or do you only get a rough idea of what the weather is going to be?
Can you check from the forecast what the weather is going to be in the place you are visiting for a day out?

The weather that comes over Britain changes so much that you must know where you are – and where you are going.
Here is a map of the regions of Britain as used on most forecasts.
1. Which region do you live in?
2. Which region is London in? (a special question for Londoners: Which region is Bristol in?)
3. Which region is Blackpool in?
4. What are the hills that make the "backbone of England" called?
5. Which region of England would first get weather coming in from the Atlantic?
6. Which region of England would first get weather coming in from the North Sea?
7. Which region of England would first get weather coming in from the south?
8. Which regions of Britain would be most sheltered by the hills from a north-east wind?

You can't stop it!

The weather moves, and changes as it goes. Huge blocks of air weighing millions and millions of tonnes move across the world. The air spins round as the air masses move along, making wind. Air masses move in different directions, and crash or mix with each other. Hills and mountains push the air higher up, where it gets colder, and so rain falls. Some air masses are more dense than others; these weigh more and are areas of HIGH PRESSURE or ANTICYCLONES; the less dense ones are areas of LOW PRESSURE or DEPRESSIONS.

Get a bucket of water and a stick. Stir it very fast. You have a model of a depression – there's a hole in the middle isn't there?
1. Which water is going round faster? The water in the middle or the water at the edge?
2. Is the slope of the depression even, or steeper in parts? Which parts?
3. Draw a cross-section of the depression.
4. Pour the water down a plug hole. Does it make another depression as it goes? This experiment gives a rough idea of how a weather depression behaves.

Forecast areas
1. Greater London
2. South-east England
3. East Anglia
4. Central Southern England
5. Midlands East
6. East England
7. Midlands West
8. Channel Islands
9. South-west England
10. South Wales
11. North Wales
12. North-west England
13. Lake District
14. Isle of Man
15. Central Northern England
16. North-east England
17. Borders
18. Edinburgh and Dundee Areas
19. Aberdeen Area
20. South-west Scotland
21. Glasgow Area
22. Central Highlands
23. Moray Firth Area
24. North-east Scotland
25. Argyll
26. North-west Scotland
27. Orkney
28. Shetland
29. Northern Ireland

141

A warm front

A cold front

An area of high pressure is made up of *either* all warm air or all cold air, and while it lasts the weather is very stable – warm air brings warm weather, cold air brings cold weather.

An area of low pressure has blocks of *both* warm air and cold air in it, and because it has both it brings very changeable weather. The blocks are as separate as the different coloured layers in Neapolitan ice cream. When a block of warm air comes, we feel a *warm front* pass; a block of cold air comes with a *cold front*. Often there is rain along the front. A warm front comes with long steady rain. A cold front comes with a hard short shower. Look at the weather map here and look at the photographs that go with it. Use the key in the margin, and complete the gaps in this grid. (If you trace just the weather symbols (not the coastline), and slide your tracing across the map until your X is over the Y on the map, you will find what the weather will be at these places in twelve hours' time.)

Weather now	Wind Direction	Wind Force	Rain or dry	Cloud amount	Temperature
Coleraine					
Renfrew					
Stockton on Tees					
London					
Weather in 12 hrs:					
Falmouth					
Bristol					
Stoke on Trent					

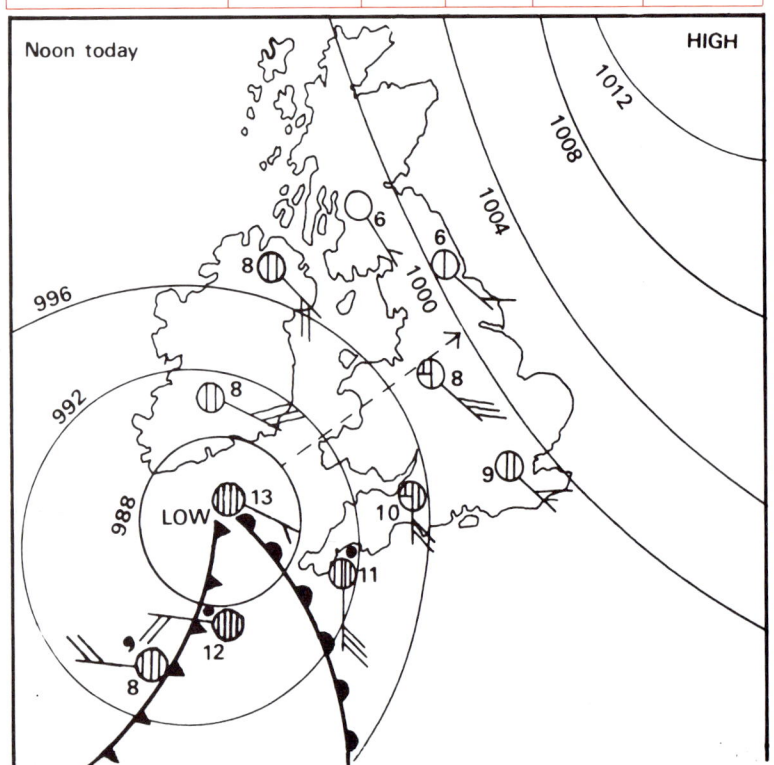

Key

- → Centre of depression expected to move as shown in 12 hrs.
- Wind direction shown by direction of arrow
- wind force shown by barbs as follows
  - short barb = force 1
  - long barb = force 2
  - long and short = force 3
  - 2 long barbs = force 4
  - and so on
- Temperature shown in °C
- Cloud cover shown in eighths of the sky covered, each half line representing one eighth covered
- ● = rain
- ❜ = showers

Lines show the 'height' or 'depth' of the pressure. This is measured in millibars.

Noon today

142

THE RADIO FORECAST

The radio forecast goes fast. Listen to a tape recording of one. Work in groups to find out what weather to expect in your own region and also another region.

Listen carefully, and each of you be responsible for remembering one part:
- the general situation
- the forecast for your area
- the forecast for the other area
- further outlook.

Next, discuss together how you will know if the weather is keeping to the expected time:
- Which way is the wind blowing?
- Will the wind change?
- What clouds can you expect?
- What temperature can you expect?

Then watch carefully during the day to see what happens. Next time discuss your results. Was the forecast correct?

How strong is the wind?
The weather forecaster usually talks of wind speeds in 'force' numbers. Here is a rough guide to give you some idea how you can feel what force the wind is:

Force 0: smoke rises vertically

Force 2: can just be felt on face

Force 4: wind lifts dust and loose paper

Force 6: large branches move

Force 8: twigs break off

Force 10: trees uprooted

NORMAL FOR THE TIME OF YEAR

Weather forecasters often say that rainfall or temperature will be normal for the time of year. What does this mean? Look up the answers to these questions in the library. You may find that the front pages of an Atlas help you most, or *Whitaker's Almanack*. Travel guides may also help.

1. Which is normally the wettest month of the year?
2. Which is the wettest part of Britain over a whole year?
3. What is the 'normal' or 'average' temperature in your district in January and in July?
4. Choose a holiday town to study. How much warmer and how much drier is it than your home district, in summer?

SPECIAL NEEDS

A full weather forecast usually mentions:
- the general situation
- whether rain is expected
- how much cloud is expected
- expected temperatures
- what winds are expected
- the visibility at sea
- with special warnings for gales, fog, frost, or snow.

What special information do these people need? Put your answers down in a grid like this:

People	Pleased to hear	Because	Worried to hear	Because

1. climber
2. arable farmer
3. holiday maker
4. fell walker
5. glider pilot
6. deep sea fisherman
7. hill farmer with sheep
8. motorist on a motorway
9. someone going shopping
10. motorist on a country lane.

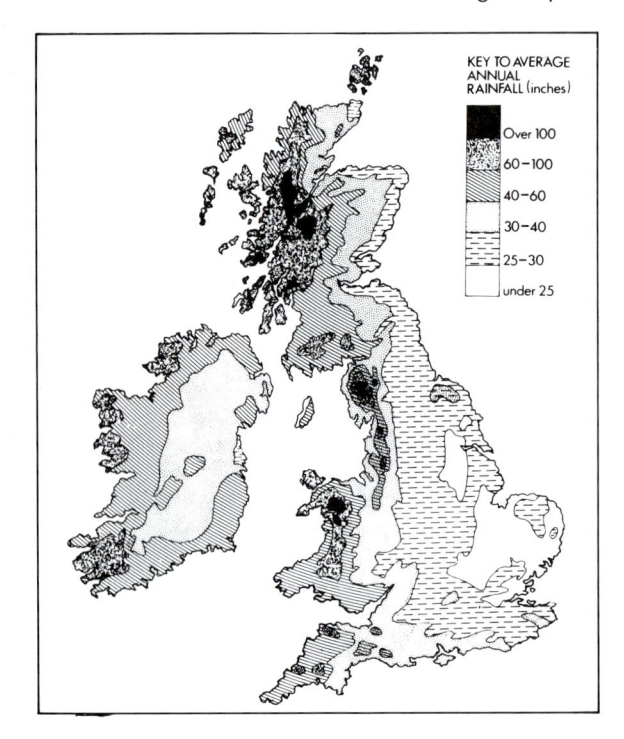

RAINFALL OVER BRITAIN

The map shows the usual pattern of rainfall over Britain during the year.

1. What is the name of the mountains in Wales where it is very wet?
2. How much rain can you expect most years at these places?
   a. Birmingham
   b. Newcastle upon Tyne
   c. Kingston upon Hull
   d. Southampton
   e. Gloucester
   f. Aberystwyth
3. What differences are there between the weather forecasts you can obtain from
   (a) the telephone (b) broadcasts
   (c) newspapers?

Weights and measures

DECIMALS

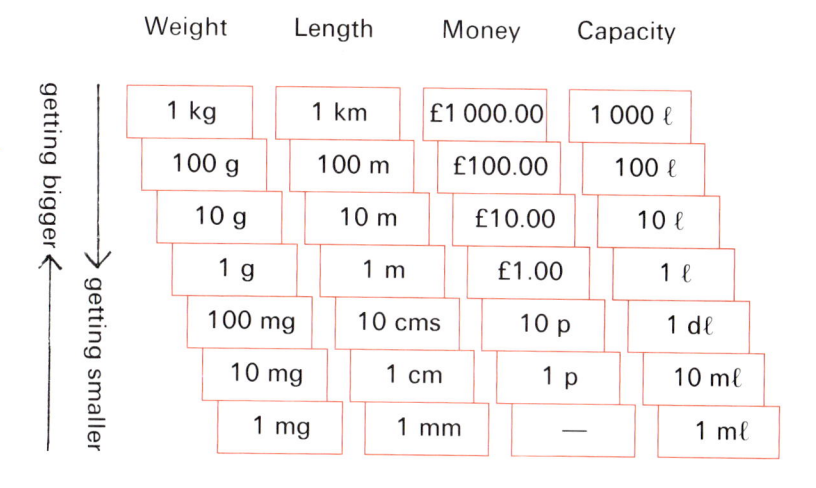

Weight	Length	Money	Capacity
1 kg	1 km	£1 000.00	1 000 ℓ
100 g	100 m	£100.00	100 ℓ
10 g	10 m	£10.00	10 ℓ
1 g	1 m	£1.00	1 ℓ
100 mg	10 cms	10 p	1 dℓ
10 mg	1 cm	1 p	10 mℓ
1 mg	1 mm	—	1 mℓ

↑ getting bigger   ↓ getting smaller

cm = centimetre
dℓ = decilitre
g = gram
kg = kilogram (kilo)
km = kilometre
£ = pound (money)

ℓ = litre
m = metre
mg = milligram
mℓ = millilitre
mm = millimetre
p = pence

A full stop on the line in among a set of digits is a decimal point.

When we read the number we call the full stop 'point' – 2.55 is read 'two point five five' (except for prices, where we say 'two pounds fifty five', although this means 'two point five five pounds').

The digits on the left of the point are whole numbers – whole grams, whole metres, and so on.

The first digit to the right of the point shows tenths of the whole gram, metre, or whatever it is.

The second digit to the right of the point shows hundredths.
The third digit to the right of the point shows thousandths.

The same quantity of something can be quoted in big measures (with decimals) or in a large number of small measures. Use the chart here to convert these quantities into other measures on the same 'ladder':

1. 10 mm = 1 ____
2. 100p = ____ 1
3. 1 000 m = 1 ____
4. 1 kg = ____ g
5. 10 dℓ = 1 ____
6. 200 cms = 2 ____
7. 400p = £____
8. 70 dℓ = ____
9. 3 000 m = ____
10. £10.00 = ____p

Use a decimal point when you give the answers to these:
11. 250 cms = 0.____
12. 250p = £____
13. 25 dℓ = ____.____ ℓ
14. 750 gms = 0.____
15. 1 100 gms = 1.____
16. 25p = £____
17. 750 mℓ = ____ ℓ
18. 1 750 mg = ____.____ g
19. 973 m = ____ km
20. 1 840 gms = ____

POUNDS AND POUNDS

There are two sorts of pound.
There is the pound in money, written £, and there is the pound in weight, which is written lb.
We are making less and less use of the pound in weight, because of metrication, but it is still to be found in some places, for example in fishing competitions, many greengrocers' shops, and on some kitchen scales (and recipe books).
A pound is divided into 16 ounces (ozs). Fourteen pounds make a stone (much used on bathroom scales), and eight stone (or 112 lbs) make a hundredweight.

16 ozs = 1 pound (lb) = about 450 grams
14 lbs = 1 stone = about 6.4 kgs
112 lbs or 8 st = 1 hundredweight (cwt) = about 50 kgs
20 cwts = 1 ton (not tonne: just a bit more)

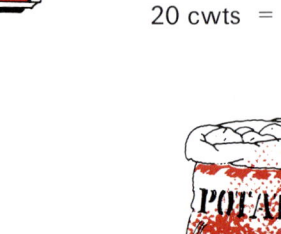

1. How many ounces are there in $\frac{1}{2}$ lb?
2. How many ounces are there in $\frac{3}{4}$ lb?
3. How many ounces are there in $1\frac{1}{4}$ lbs?
4. Which is heavier, 100 lbs or 1 cwt?
5. Which is heavier, 32 ozs or 2 lbs 2 ozs?
6. Which is heavier, 500 grams or 16 ounces?
7. Which is heavier, 13 kgs or 35 lbs?
8. How many grams are there in 2 kgs?
9. How many grams are there in 2.3 kgs?
10. Which is heavier, 0.5 kgs or 1 lb?
11. Who is heavier, Craig who weighs 6 stone 7 lbs, or Christopher, who weighs 43 kgs?
12. Claire weighs 47 kgs. How much more is that than Caroline's weight of 6 stone 13 lbs?
13. What is the total weight, in kilos and grams, of these loads of shopping?

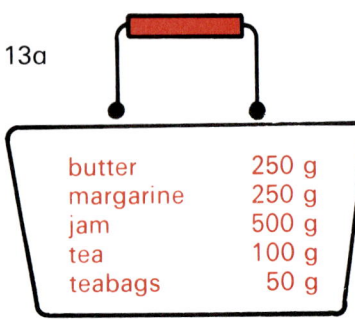

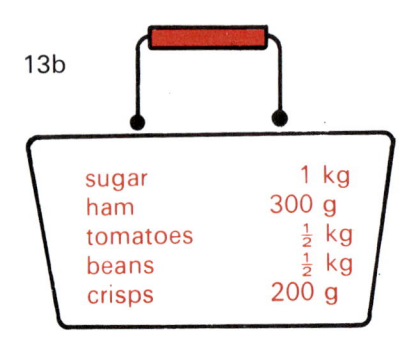

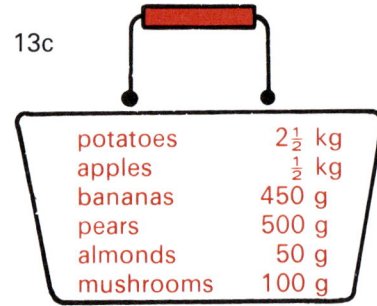

13a
butter	250 g
margarine	250 g
jam	500 g
tea	100 g
teabags	50 g

13b
sugar	1 kg
ham	300 g
tomatoes	$\frac{1}{2}$ kg
beans	$\frac{1}{2}$ kg
crisps	200 g

13c
potatoes	$2\frac{1}{2}$ kg
apples	$\frac{1}{2}$ kg
bananas	450 g
pears	500 g
almonds	50 g
mushrooms	100 g

INCHES, FEET AND YARDS

When we measure things in Britain these days, we sometimes use metric measures (cm, m, km) and sometimes the old *imperial* measures (inches, feet, yards, and miles).

In general conversation we have kept to the old measures – snow is so many inches deep, a wall is so many feet high. These words are likely to stay in use for a long time.

The old measurements will stay in some places. Most homes have rulers and tapes marked in inches and feet; bricks in the walls that measure 3 inches × 6 inches × 9 inches; window frames made of wood 2 inches or $2\frac{1}{2}$ inches thick and so on.

Timber yards sell timber that is measured as so many *metres* long but so many *inches* across. Some timber yards even use a measure called a *metric foot* which is neither a foot nor a metre.

It is usual to convert inches into feet if you have more than 12, and common to convert feet into yards if you have more than 3 (particularly for higher numbers).

1 inch (1 in) (1″)		= about $2\frac{1}{2}$ cms
12 inches (12 ins) (12″)	= 1 foot (1 ft) (1′)	= about 30 cms
3 feet (3 ft) (3′)	= 1 yard (1 yd)	= about 914 cms
1 760 yards (1 760 yds)	= 1 mile (1 m)	= about 1.6 kms

Work out the figures you need to complete this table showing the lengths of pieces of material, wood, or carpet that you might have measured:

Question	Lengths measured	Total number of pieces	Total length (imp.)	Rough metric conversion

1 3″, 4″, 5″, 4″, 6″, 7″, 6″, 8″, 5″
2 1 ft 3″, 2 ft 4″, 4 ft 3″, 5 ft 2″, 2 ft.
3 2 yds 2 ft 1″, 2 yds 1 ft 9 ins, 1 yd 2 ft 3 ins, 4 yds 2 ft 11″
4 4 yds 3 ft 2 ins, 2 yds, 2 ft $3\frac{1}{2}$″, 1 yd 2 ft $2\frac{1}{2}$ ins, 1 yd 1 ft 1″
5 5 yds 2 ft 6 ins, 3 yds 2 ft 3 ins, 2 yds 1 ft $3\frac{1}{2}$″, 4′ 2″

TAKE YOUR OWN MEASUREMENTS

Try taking the following measurements of these things on both metric and imperial scales:

Question	Item	Imperial measurement	Metric measurement

1 Your own height
2 Your own waistline
3 Your own collar size
4 Friend's height
5 Friend's waistline
6 Friend's collar size
7 Tabletop: length
8 Tabletop: width
9 Bookcase: length
10 Bookcase shelf width
11 Bricks in wall: length
12 Bricks in wall: height
13 Nail or screw: length
14 Head of nut or bolt
15 Floor tile: width

METRIC LENGTHS

Nowadays, we are all getting used to measuring in metres (m). A thousand metres is a kilometre (km).

Metres can be divided into a hundred parts. Each part is a centimetre (cm).

And each centimetre can be divided into ten small parts. Each smaller part is a millimetre (mm).

Write down in digits:
1. Six point four kilometres
2. Eight point three six metres
3. Four point one centimetres
4. Twenty eight point five kilometres
5. Twelve point three four eight kilometres.

Write down in words, and also convert into mm and write in digits:
6. 14.73 cms
7. 1 m 14 cms
8. 1.143 m
9. 1 km 350 m
10. 1.436 kms.

DEGREES

There are two sorts of degree you can measure. These are degrees of angle and degrees of temperature. Both are written with a ° above the line like this: 10°.

There are 360° in a complete turn, including a compass.

N
W   E
S

A quarter turn (sharp corner) is 90° which is called a right angle, and a half turn is 180°.

Temperature is usually measured in °C (Centigrade) or °F (Fahrenheit).

1. Which of the measurements of either sort of degree would you expect to hear in:
   a. a builder's yard?
   b. a hospital?
   c. a kitchen?
   d. allotment gardens? (Plants may be killed by frost)
2. If you measure the angle of a shelf and find it is 85°, what problems might arise?
3. If you look at the thermometer in your deep freeze and find it says 33° F, what would you do?
4. If you find that someone's temperature is 38.2° C, what would you advise?
5. What happens if you make a pot of tea with water that has reached 200° F?

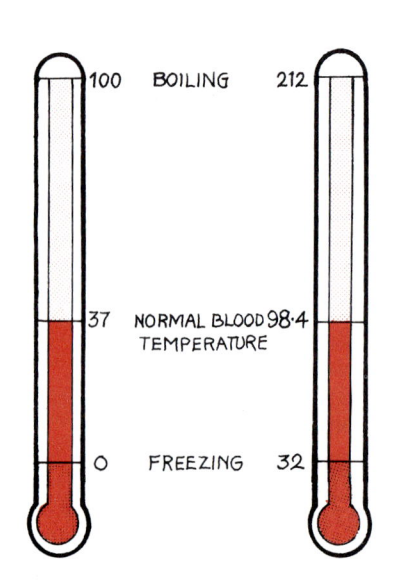

148

What about fractions?

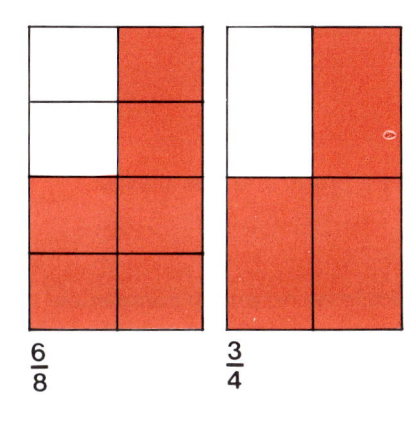

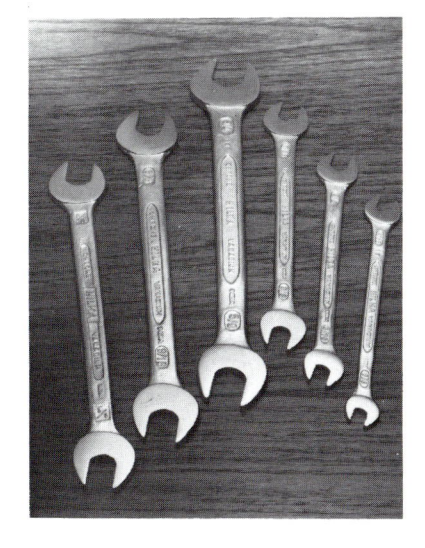

WORKING WITH FRACTIONS

One in four (people are under 20) can be written

one
in   = ¼ = a quarter
four

Nine out of ten (people are kind) can be written

nine
out of   = 9/10 = nine tenths
ten

Six out of eight

six
out of   = 6/8 = six eighths
eight

is the same proportion as three out of four

three
out of   = ¾ = three quarters
four

Fractions with special names are half (½), quarters (¼ ¾) and thirds (⅓ ⅔).

All other fractions are read as they are written, for example four fifths (⅘) or three sixteenths (3/16).

1. Write these fractions in digits:
   (a) one eighth   (b) one twelfth   (c) one fourteenth
   (d) two ninths   (e) six sevenths (f) eleven twelfths

2. Write these fractions in words:
   (a) 1/10 (b) 3/10 (c) 5/12 (d) 7/12 (e) ¾ (f) 3/8

3. Use a ruler to meaure a variety of objects in fractions of an inch or centimetres. Measure the same object on different scales – you may find something that is ¼ inch across, and then you should also find it is 2/8, 3/12 and 4/16 inches across. You will need to be very exact with your measurements, and if something does not fit exactly you should put + or −, or leave it out altogether. Suitable objects to measure would be:
   a width of pencil   b width of two pencils
   c width of 1p coin   d width of 2p coin
   e width of ruler   f width of pencil sharpener

4. Lawrence had a bad day with his spanners; every time he picked one up, it was just one size too small.
   What were the sizes he needed each time?
   (always add 1/16 inch to each size)

   (a) ¾ inch   (b) 7/8 inch   (c) ¼ inch   (d) 7/16 inch
   (e) 9/16 inch (f) 11/16 inch (g) ½ inch   (h) 3/8 inch

5. Some butter packets are marked with lines so that you can cut the right weight without going to the trouble of weighing it. If a packet is marked with fifths, and contains 250 gms of butter altogether, how much butter is cut off if you cut

   a at the third line and keep the big end,
   b at the third line and keep the small end,
   c at the first line and keep the big end,
   d at the fourth line and only keep the small end.

6/8

3/4

149

Will you get the job?

PHONING FOR A JOB?

Stop and think who wants what:

You probably want:
good pay
a job that will last
friendly work
a pleasant place to work
Do you also want these? (Some people don't – why not?)
interesting work?
training?
good holidays?
overtime?
responsibility?
opportunities for promotion?

The Personnel Manager wants:
your skill, so that the firm can make a profit; and that means:
willingness
hard work
punctuality
If firms didn't make profits there would be no public companies to work for.
Places that aren't there to make profits (corporation parks department, fire service, police) still need to balance their accounts.

Know your English!
Before you phone the Personnel Manager, make sure you know what all these words mean. They are part of his daily English and he'll be surprised if you don't understand them:

closed shop	time off
canteen	managing director
clocking in	union
block release	luncheon voucher
teabreak	insurance card
day release	foreman
shop steward	shop floor

(Words to do with Unions are explained on p. 121.)

Translate your English!
Here are some words from school that would sound funny at work. What are the right words when you are at work? The answers are all in the list above.

Draw this grid on your paper and fill in the gaps. Can you think of any more "pairs" like this?

at school	at work
holidays	
break	
dining hall	
registration	
headmaster	
absence	

YOUNG PERSON WANTED

Play-reading

Parts: Personnel Manager: a stern, solemn middle aged man. He thinks all young people should want to work hard for 44 hours a week; never smoke; have eight O levels; and call older men "Sir".
Telephone Receptionist: She gets about one call every minute of every day, and has 130 different extensions to put the callers through to. She likes to smoke 30 a day on the job.
Trudy: a pupil about to leave school.
Tina: another pupil about to leave school.
(You can add some more applicants if you like).

Scene: This advertisement appeared in the local paper:

YOUNG PERSON WANTED
for secretarial work

Good pay, easy hours, pleasant working conditions, good prospects.
Apply to Personnel Manager, Smith's of High St.
Telephone 84307

Trudy: *(thinking aloud as she dials)* Eight four three oh seven. Sounds a good job. Bet I get it. Quick off the mark. That'll be a laugh in school. First one in the class with a job. Yes, it's ringing.

Recept: *(quickly and mechanically)* Smith's of High Street. What number?

Trudy: *(caught out: she hadn't expected this)* Can't hear you.

Recept: *(fed up)* What extension do you want?

Trudy: *(getting flustered)* What? Is that Smith's of High Street?

Recept: I told you so. Who do you want?

Trudy: I want that job in the paper. You know, the secretarial one. Can I have it? I hope I'm the first one. My school will give me a good report.

Recept: You want the Personnel Manager then?

Trudy: I thought you were.

Recept: I'll put you through.

(Trudy hears another ring).

Pers. Man: Yes?

Trudy: Is that Smith's of High Street?

P.M. *(sharply)* Personnel Manager speaking.

Trudy: Oh, it's me. About that job. The one in the paper. Can I have it? What's the pay?

P.M. *(crossly)* Are you applying for a job in this factory?

Trudy: Yes, the one in the paper.

P.M. We had eight advertisements in the paper today young lady. Which one are you talking about?

Trudy: The secretary. Good pay and easy hours. Can I start at half past nine? I hate getting up in the mornings. What's the pay and when can I begin?

P.M. *(coldly)* If you would send me a letter of application with your name and address and the name of a referee I will arrange an interview in due course. Thank you for your call. Good morning. *(Puts down the phone)*

Trudy: Now what? It's gone dead. What's a letter of applic – application was it? Heck!

Tina: *(thinking aloud)* Eight four three oh seven. I wonder what it's like. I hope I get an interview.

Recept:	Smith's of High Street. What number?
Tina:	Personnel Manager please.
Recept:	Putting you through.
P.M.	*(who has just had shop steward coming in threatening to stop the production line)* Personnel Manager speaking.
Tina:	Oh good morning Sir. My name is Tina Groves and I'm enquiring about the secretarial job advertised today.
P.M.	Good. Could you come for an interview – let's see – tomorrow at 2.30?
Tina:	Yes thank you, Sir, that'll suit me fine.
P.M.	Good morning, Miss Groves.
Tina:	Good morning, Sir.

Look up some advertisements

Now look up some advertisements in your local paper. Try to make up a short play of the same type that will fit the details in the advertisement. You might like to add some of the points below.

GOING FOR AN INTERVIEW

When you go for an interview you have a right to find out about your possible work place too – it is not just the Personnel Manager who should ask all the questions. But be careful how you say what you want to say – and choose the right time too.

Which of these are the best ways of asking the questions? Which questions are good ones to ask? Two of these would be rather silly if you are going for your first job – which two?

How much are you going to pay me?
What is the rate of pay?
How long do I have to work?
What are the hours?
Do I get dinner free?
What are the canteen arrangements?
Do you have a pension scheme?
How long are the holidays?
What are the holiday arrangements?
Do you make redundancy payments?
Do I have to go to College?
Do I get day release or block release?

Wiring three-pin plugs

Mains electricity can kill.
Be careful.
Always disconnect any electrical equipment before you make any repair or adjustment to it.

You may need to put a three-pin plug on a new piece of equipment.
You may need to put a new fuse in an old plug.
You may find an old plug is getting hot – if it does, it needs rewiring.

THREE CORE FLEXES

The electric wire for a heater, kettle or iron has three separate wires inside it.
Each of these three wires is wrapped in a covering to *insulate* it – to keep the electricity in where it is meant to be.
One of these wires is coloured BROWN. This wire is LIVE, taking the electricity into the plug, and so to the machine you are wiring up. This wire must be joined to a FUSE, which controls how much electricity can get in.
Another wire is coloured BLUE. This wire is 'neutral' – and takes the electricity out of the equipment again, completing the circuit.
The third wire is YELLOW AND GREEN. This is the EARTH and is the escape route for the electricity if something goes wrong.

Choosing the right fuse

There are two ways of measuring how much electricity you have got.
You can measure it in AMPS, which is like saying how much force you get when you turn a water tap on – a few amps would be like a quiet trickle of water, and a lot of amps would be like a sudden rush of water.
You can measure it in VOLTS, which is like saying how big the pipe is that carries the water to your tap.
Mains electricity usually comes to us at something between 220 and 240 volts, and we don't usually alter this at home (except in transformers for car battery chargers and model trains).
But the machines we use need different numbers of amps.
The strongest fuse you would use at home is the 13 amp fuse.
You need this for electric heaters and kettles. You do not need so much for many other machines.
If the label on a machine says you should use a fuse for only 3 amps, 5 amps, or 7 amps, it is silly to use one for 13 amps.
You are more likely to ruin your machine, and perhaps hurt yourself.
You can buy a packet of fuses in any electrician's.
The fuse clips straight into its socket in the plug.

Getting ready to wire up

You need to begin by preparing the flex you are going to use.
You will need about 2 cms of each of the three wires cut free from each other. Cut the outer cover carefully back 2 cms with wire strippers or scissors. Then strip the insulation off each.

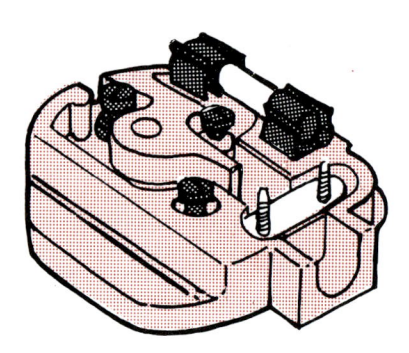

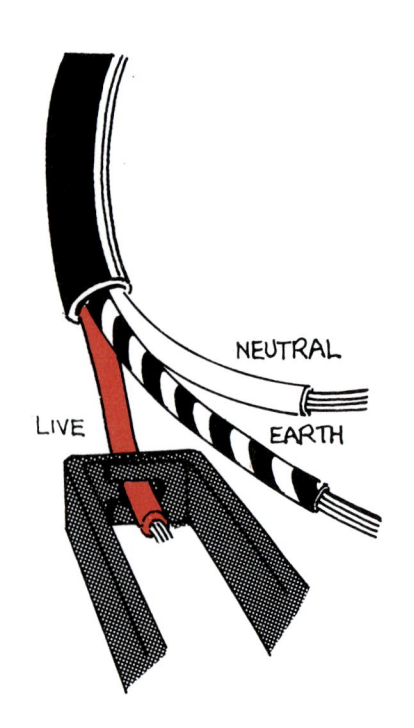

WITHOUT CUTTING ANY OF THE WIRE INSIDE. If you have a pair of wire strippers this will make it much easier, otherwise you will have to use scissors and score round the insulation carefully, and then pull it off with your fingers.

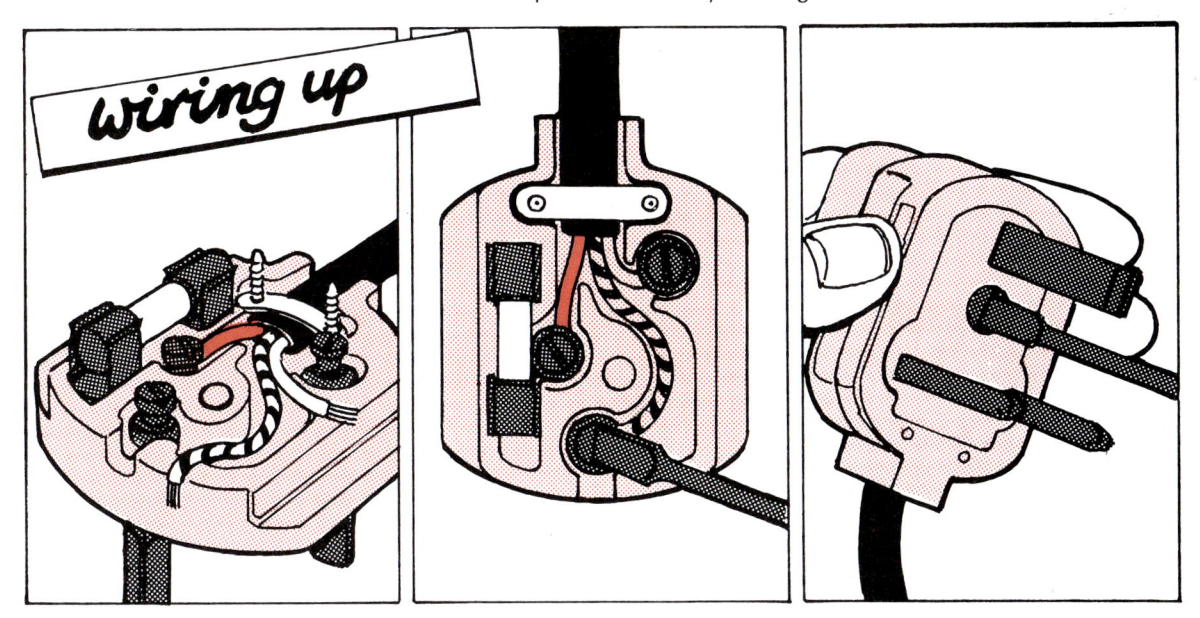

wiring up

1. Remember to run the flex under the cord grip at the bottom of the plug before you fit any of the wires. It is very important that you check that each wire goes in its right hole. With some plugs you may need to lift out the fuse while you wire up the live wire.

2. Screw each wire down really tight, so it cannot be pulled out again. Make sure that all your wires inside are neat and tidy, and that there are no loose threads from one wire getting anywhere near threads from another wire – these could spark across. There should be no loose threads inside at all.

3. Screw the cover on again. Test.

CHECK THE PLUGS

Can you wire a three-pin plug well? Work in pairs and check each other's plugs with care.

Mark the job out of ten. Take marks off for each of the following faults:

Any wire in the wrong place – take off 10.
Any bare wire touching another wire – take off 10.
Any screw loose – take off 1.
Insulation stripped too far back, wire showing – take off 1.
Insulation cut too deep – wire thinned – take off 1.
Insulating cord not inside grip – take off 1.
Wire sticking out on far side of screw – take off 2.
Wires twisted or bent – take off 1.
Any other fault – at least 1 (explain the fault).

Don't be satisfied until you score $\frac{10}{10}$ and don't use any plug that has scored less than $\frac{10}{10}$.

155

Work experience

You may be given a chance to take part in a Work Experience scheme. Will it be a success? Will it be just time off school, or a time when you really learn something about what it is like in a work place?

Here is a list of comments made by three students who had been on Work Experience. The arrangements for Work Experience schemes vary. These students had worked the same hours as all the other workers for two complete weeks, and had not been back to school during that time. Sort these out so that the right comments by the Personnel Manager, supervisor and teacher go with the comments that each student made.

THE PERSONNEL MANAGER REPORTED:

One student took great interest, was always punctual, worked very hard, and should apply for the next vacancy at the firm, or quote the firm as a referee if applying for a job elsewhere.
Another student was satisfactory.
The third student was late every morning, and had to be spoken to about personal appearance.

The Supervisor reported:
One student was cheeky, made a lot of mistakes, and upset the regular workers so much that a complaint was made to the Union.
Another student seemed very shy, did each job all right but never spoke up when the job was done.
Another student was easy to get on with, quick on the uptake, and a very accurate worker.

THE TEACHER REPORTED:

One student had no questions when visited, and said there was no problem about the work.
Another student, when visited, was hard at work, and explained what was going on clearly.
Another student, when visited, was at teabreak, and could not explain what the day's work had been.

THE STUDENTS TOLD THEIR FRIENDS:

One student said that Work Experience was boring, sorting stock out all day. 'My Dad is going to complain about it'.
Another student said it was great. No school for two weeks! 'And you just doss around until the supervisor comes by!'
Another student said it was hard work. 'I was flaked out each evening.'

SUMMING UP WORK EXPERIENCE

Which of these statements might be true about Work Experience? Say if you think each of these might be true or false, and in each case make a comment about how you think you would feel.
1. The regular workers are pleased to have you do their jobs, so they could put their feet up and yet get the same pay.
2. It is easier to go on doing one's own job than to explain it to a Work Experience student.

3   It makes a dull job interesting to have to explain it.
4   We're on piece work and there's no way we will have Work Experience students coming in and slowing us down.
5   There's no difference between going on Work Experience and doing a Saturday job.
6   Teachers are just like everyone else and treat you the same, expect the same things, and explain things in the same way as anyone at a work place.
7   The way to make a success of Work Experience is to be observant, ask good questions, show enthusiasm and be adaptable.
8   It's quite different being in a work place for a whole week and working their hours.
9   Everyone is pleased to see Work Experience students and will help them as much as possible.
10 The best thing to do on Work Experience is to keep quiet and just do what you are told.
11 If things go wrong with the arrangements on Work Experience you just have to grin and bear it.
12 One of the best things about Work Experience is being able to talk to a wide variety of people about work.
13 There is a great difference between school-based work experience lasting about two weeks, and Work Experience with Y.T.S. lasting for six months.
14 Employers like to have six month Work Experience workers as a form of cheap labour.

TAKEN FOR A RIDE?

Going into a work place involves more experiences than just changing your timetable in school. Have you thought about the range of situations and problems that could arise any time while you are there?

Cast
Jean Wilson
Jeff Wrightson } Three students on a Work Experience scheme
Sheila Stevens
Miss Roberts, secretary to managing director, aged 48, slim, tall, sharp features.
Fred, the supervisor, aged 50
Susan, aged 18
Jenny, aged 25
John, aged 19 } employees of the firm
Tony, aged 18
Sally, aged 20

Scene is a large retailing and wholesaling firm dealing in D.I.Y. and builders' supplies. There are several separate buildings of various ages around a large car park and yard.
At the firm, 8.00 a.m. Monday. Supervisor's office.

Supervisor   'Ere we are then. Ready for a day's work? Just sit there a moment. Then I'll take you up and you can get started. – Hey! Tony! Got that big order that came in on Friday? Here's a kid what'll help you with it. What's your name?

Jean	Jean.
Supervisor	O.K. Jeanie, off you go with Tony then. You'll be with him this week. – And *your* names?
Jeff	Jeff.
Sheila	Sheila.
Supervisor	Come along with me then. I'll get you two working in the office this week.

(They walk upstairs and along the corridors.)

Supervisor	Mornin' Miss Roberts. I've got some help for you this week. A couple of kids in on one of these school visit things.
Sheila	*(whispers to Jeff)* Oh no! She lives up my street. She's awful.
Miss Roberts	*(coldly, to supervisor)* So I see.
Supervisor	There's another kid down with Tony. She can come up here next week and I'll put these two with him.

(Supervisor goes.)

Miss Roberts	What are your names then?
Jeff	Jeff.
Miss Roberts	Speak up!
Jeff	Jeff.
Miss Roberts	Jeff *what*?
Jeff	Jeff Wrightson.
Miss Roberts	Jeff Wilson?
Jeff	No, Wrightson.
Miss Roberts	Oh, Wrightson. Any relation of Sarah Wrightson?
Jeff	Yes, she's my great-aunt.
Miss Roberts	O.K., I'll have a word with her if I catch you mucking around. And you? Your name? I've seen you before.
Sheila	Sheila Stevens. You live down my street.
Miss Roberts	I think *you* live down *my* street young lady. O.K., Sheila, you're on switchboard today. Come along!

(They go. Jeff is left standing, and doesn't know what to do. The door opens. A couple of young girls come in.)

Susan	Well, what do you know? It's Jeff! What are you doing here?

Jeff	Work Experience. I didn't know you worked here.
Susan	Started a month ago. Nice to see you. Where are you working then?
Jeff	Don't know. Miss – Miss Roberts was it? – she's just left me standing here.
Susan	Well, I'm on Post. Pop down and see me. I'll get along now before Miss R comes back.
Jeff	What's she like?
Susan	She's awful. Keep out of her way and you'll be O.K. See you then.

(She goes off, talking with her friend Sally. We hear voices fade as they walk down the corridor.)

Sally	Who's that then?
Susan	Lad I know.
Sally	Thought you went out with John?
Susan	What's that got to do with it?

(They disappear. Miss Roberts returns to Jeff).

Miss Roberts	Come along with me then, boy. You're on Post this week. Lots of walking about. Don't go wasting time. I expect you to get on with it and not hang around talking. Understand?
Jeff	Yes, Miss.
Miss Roberts	*(correcting him)* Miss Roberts.
Jeff	Yes, Miss Roberts.
Miss Roberts	Jenny, there's a boy to help you this week. Let me know if he gets in your way. Don't let him slow you down at all. I want that post out by 9 o'clock just as usual.
Jenny	Yes, Miss Roberts.

(Miss Roberts goes.)

Susan	Well, I'll be blowed!
Jenny	What's up?
Susan	Fancy her putting Jeff in here!
Jenny	Know him then?
Susan	Sure I do! Hey, Jeff, I'm taking this post down to old Sarah in the accounts office. Coming?
Jeff	Not her! She's my great-aunt!
Susan	What a laugh! Come on!

(They go. Miss Roberts comes back just as the phone rings. She picks it up.)

Miss Roberts	Yes?
Sheila's voice	Who is it?
Miss Roberts	It's Miss Roberts and I'm in the Post Room. What do you want?
Sheila's voice	Oh, sorry, I had a customer calling.
Miss Roberts	Well, get it right then. Put the call through to the Orders Department.

(She slams the phone down, and speaks to Jenny.)

Miss Roberts	These kids! They muck everything up. Don't see why we have to have them.
Jenny	Yes, Miss Roberts.
Miss Roberts	Keep them busy and watch what they're doing.
Jenny	Yes, Miss Roberts.

(Miss Roberts goes. Susan and Jeff return.)

Jenny	Keep the noise down! Miss Roberts is about.

	Here's the pile for Fred in the warehouse. Both going?
Susan	You bet!

(They go to the warehouse. As they approach they overhear the end of a conversation between Tony and Jean.)

Tony	Well, it's only fair. After all, they're not paying you are they? And no one will notice the difference.
Jean	Yes, I see.

(Tony goes. Jean meets Susan and Jeff.)

Jean	Watch-yer, Jeff.
Jeff	How's things?
Jean	Great! *(whispers)* Want any stuff tonight? Tony's been telling me how to work the system.
Jeff	Work the system?
Jean	You know, fix the orders. You can slip in a bit here and there and they'll never know. Want anything?
Jeff	They'll search you on the way out.
Jean	I know *that*! Tony's told me how to miss it. Want anything?
Jeff	I'll let you know.
Susan	Come on, we'd better get the rest of the post done before Miss R checks up. She's on the warpath today. Monday morning.

(Back in the post room.)

Jenny	Last two lots then. Susan, you take that lot to the Manager's office, and Jeff, here's another pile for the warehouse that you missed just now.

(Jeff goes with post to the warehouse. On the way, a big lad steps out in front of him.)

John	You that kid that came down here with the post just now?
Jeff	Yep.
John	What were you doing along with Sue?
Jeff	I'm on Post with her. Anyway, I know her.
John	Know her? What do you mean then?
Jeff	She's a friend of mine.
John	Now look here, she's my girl. You get yourself on another job and lay off her. See?
Jeff	I didn't ask to go on Post. Miss Roberts sent me.
John	Well, you go and ask for a change.
Jeff	I can't! And why should I? Sue's my girl. I've known her for ages.
John	I'll punch your head in for that!

(John starts fighting. They fall back into stacks of double glazing units. All the units fall and break. The boys are still fighting when the supervisor comes up.)

Supervisor	What the hell are you playing at? Pack it in. Off you both go to the boss. Quick! Scram!

(They go. The day passes. Later, we find Jean sat by a big box of bolts, counting them one by one. Tony comes in.)

Sheila's voice	Is Jean there?
Jean	Hello, who is it?
Sheila	It's me. Do you know, Jeff's in trouble. The boss has sent him home.

Jean	I know. I heard about it. Had a scrap didn't he?
Sheila	Yes, smashed up piles of stuff. Must have been great.
(Miss Roberts' voice is heard from Sheila's end)	What are you doing? Talking to your friends? That's not allowed on switchboard duties.
(Sheila's voice is heard over the phone)	But it's after school hours. I'm not really at work any more.
Miss R's voice	Aren't you? Why not? We are.
Sheila's voice	You're not paying us. You can't make us work after four o'clock.
Miss R's voice	Don't speak to me like that, young lady. You do what you're told here.
Sheila's voice	Well, I'm going then.
Miss R's voice	And don't come back! People in this place don't knock off at four like you kids. – Jenny, get me the Comprehensive School on the line please.

(The phone goes dead, and Jean puts it down. Fred comes in.)
(She goes.)

(Supervisor rings gatehouse)	Pete? That young lass from school. Just check her pockets for her will you? Ta.
Supervisor	Jenny? One more call before you knock off. Can you get me the Comprehensive School please?

1. When did the three students each not feel particularly happy?
2. What signs are there that students on Work Experience are not welcome to the employees, even though the Personnel Manager may be happy about the scheme?
3. What signs are there that students in Work Experience are not respected, both in ways in which they are spoken to and how they are treated?
4. What was the correct approach to the managing director's secretary and who used it?
5. Why might dishonest people in a work place be pleased to make use of a student? What is a 'fall guy'?
6. What did the students do or say that was wrong?

Writing a formal letter

Most of the letters you are going to need to write are likely to be 'business' letters. And you will get better answers if you send good letters.

Read through these pupils' letters carefully. Notice:
- Where they have put their addresses
- Where they have put the date
- How they have set out what they wanted to say
- The words they chose for saying it

Then write similar letters of your own, using your own address and today's date. Some ideas are given below each letter.

> 7 Calamity Park
> Broughton in
> Furness,
> Cumbria
> LA20 6YZ
>
> Sunday 25 September, 1983
>
> Dear Sir or Madam,
>
> Quotation for moped insurance
>
> Could you please send me a quotation for comprehensive insurance for a moped? I will be 16 in a month's time, and would like full cover. I am planning to buy a second hand 49 c.c. machine that will cost me £350.
> My friend Jasmine Plant, who has had insurance arranged through your office for the last four years, suggested that I should contact you for a quotation.
> Since I am a teetotaller, is it possible to be given special rates?
>
> Yours faithfully,
> Sherie Beer.
>
> The manager,
> Profitable Insurance brokers Ltd.
> 44 Redpenny Road, ANNAN,
> Dumfriesshire
> DG12 5SA

1. Write a letter of your own asking for some form of insurance.
2. Write a letter of your own asking for a brochure or catalogue.

29 Cliff Street
Edinburgh
EH9 3TA

Monday 12 December 1983.

Dear Sir or Madam,
    Could you please send me details of the Union for a project I am doing at school.

    I am interested to know something about the history of the Union and the services that are offered to its members. I would also like to know what the present membership fee is and how one can join.

    I have been interested in the activities of Unions since attending the Durham Miners Gala last year and I am working on a project to do with the effect of Unions on the working conditions in the country.

Yours faithfully

Li How Yen

The Branch Secretary
National Union of
        Workers
9 Pillar Box Street
London
WC2E 6EP.

---

35 Airport Road
CROYDON
CR0 9UR

Tuesday 19 July 1983
Dear Sir or Madam
    <u>Your ref: LCD 1983 - 0342 - 02</u>
The calculator enclosed with this letter was sent to me in error. My order of June 13th asked you to send me on approval a "Brainwave" Home Computer ref. no. LCD-1983.

    I was particularly anxious to receive the computer quickly and was disappointed to find that an error had been made. I would be grateful if you would do all you can to make sure the computer is sent as quickly as possible.

Sales Dept.,   Yours faithfully,
Silicon Sums PLC   Peter Key
127 Billside Road, CARLISLE
CA1 2FJ

3 Write a letter of your own that is returning something that has been sent to you in error.
4 Write a letter of your own that is politely complaining about a fault in something you have been sent.

5. Write a letter of your own making a general enquiry of this sort about the possibility of work.
6. Write a letter of your own applying for a job that has been advertised.

---

17 Bleek Road
West Wickham
Kent
BR4 9RT

Tuesday 18 January 1983

Dear Sir or Madam,

<u>Vacancies for School Leavers</u>

Will there be any vacancies in the shop for school leavers this year? I am 16, and will be leaving school in May

I would particularly like to work in retailing as I have had a Saturday job for the last ten months at the supermarket, and my uncle has a small shop of his own in Pudsey I always enjoy meeting people in the shop and I am keen to learn more about window dressings

I have not been in any teams at school and do not expect to do very well in the examinations, but I always help with the stage set when there is a production, and I help with selling the tickets.

Yours faithfully,

Yoki Owesetu

The Personnel Manager,
The Greatest Department Store,
72 Equity Street
LONDON
WC1A 4U67

Note to the teacher

THE USE OF THIS BOOK

This is not a course book to be followed in order from beginning to end. It is a book to be picked up as and when the need arises, so that reference can be made to the specific skills that are wanted at that moment. The material presented for each skill breaks into self-contained sections, and it is anticipated that those who find a skill easy will complete all the sections in the time that others need to master the rudiments. The book is backed up by its companion, *Practice in Basic Skills*, by a set of Spirit Masters, and supplemented by *English You Need*.

While some schools may want to teach a specific Basic Skills course others may want to use these books in general Humanities or English courses, or Rosla, general examination and non-examination courses, or in a wide variety of other settings.

Why teach Basic Skills?
Underlying this course is the philosophy that when your pupils are approaching school leaving age those who have not found conventional academic work easy, need something much more worldly, more practical and more varied than just going on with academic subjects. Basic Skills do not replace these subjects: they belong alongside them. Basic Skills are not provided purely to pander to adolescent taste: they are urgently needed if our pupils are to be considered educated when they leave school. Every skill here is one that may well be called on in the first weeks out at work, and if the pupil has not mastered it at school he or she may well be exposed to ridicule in the crueller world outside – 'What do they teach you at school these days? Don't you even know how to . . .' Although every skill here could be classified under the usual school subject headings, in practice many are often missed – or, at least, the pupils miss them. The fortunate pupils acquire them from home or by their own devices; other pupils need more specific help which is all too often lacking.

It is essential that the skills remain firmly tied to the real world, and to achieve this, class sizes must be kept small. It is possible to teach larger groups, but the essential practical work and the visits become very difficult to arrange then. This is a course about things that are really needed, and the work should be as real as possible. At Dorcan School we teach Basic Skills by adopting a theme for a series of lessons, and then linking a number of skills with it. The series of lessons usually includes at least one visit or practical activity. Understanding and retention is greatly enhanced when a practical involvement of this sort is included.

BASIC SKILLS AT DORCAN SCHOOL, SWINDON

'Skills' appears as an option for fourth and fifth year pupils among the other options. It leads to a C.S.E. examination (full range of grades) for those who wish to take it at this level. Skills has been taught at the school since 1974, and up to five groups per year group have been timetabled for it. The usual allocation is about two and a half hours a week, although more time would be very useful.

The examination has six elements of assessment. Three are examination papers; two relatively conventional papers, but also one which is based on a 'Mystery Tour', where the candidates are taken to a town or city they hardly know, and on arrival are given a question paper with things to find out about employment opportunities, leisure activities, special features of the town and so on. After a morning collecting information in the town, they return to write up their results under examination conditions. The other elements of the assessment include two areas of course work presented as topics, and an oral in which the emphasis is on 'Could you tell someone else how to do ...'

RESOURCES

Effective teaching of Skills demands the accumulation of a good stock of resources, many of which can be collected at no cost: old telephone directories, old A.A. and R.A.C. Handbooks, gardening catalogues, timetables and leaflets, travel agents' booklets, advertisements posted through the door, forms of all types and so on. Jumble sales are an excellent source of much other stock, such as books to read to young children, 'do it yourself' manuals and manuals for various types of car. With care and forethought, the amount of stock that has to be bought new may be limited to items such as medical thermometers, electrical screwdrivers and plugs, and standard items of school stock.

Thomas Nelson and Sons Ltd
Nelson House Mayfield Road
Walton-on-Thames Surrey
KT12 5PL UK

51 York Place
Edinburgh
EH1 3JD UK

Thomas Nelson (Hong Kong) Ltd
Toppan Building 10/F
22A Westlands Road
Quarry Bay Hong Kong

Distributed in Australia by

Thomas Nelson Australia
480 La Trobe Street
Melbourne Victoria 3000
and in Sydney, Brisbane, Adelaide
and Perth

© Humphrey Dobinson 1983
First published by Thomas Nelson and Sons
Ltd 1983
ISBN 0-17-433392-7
NPN 9 8 7 6 5 4

All Rights Reserved. This publication is
protected in the United Kingdom by the
Copyright Act 1956 and in other countries by
comparable legislation. No part of it may be
reproduced or recorded by any means without
the permission of the publisher. This
prohibition extends (with certain very limited
exceptions) to photocopying and similar
processes, and written permission to make a
copy or copies must therefore be obtained
from the publisher in advance. It is advisable
to consult the publisher if there is any doubt
regarding the legality of any proposed
copying.

Printed in Hong Kong

Acknowledgements

Mike Abrahams/Network: page 139, Aerofilms: pages 18, 26, Chris Alderman: pages 10, 16, 52, 67 (bottom), 69, 80, 90, 94, 110, 112, 119, 137, 147, 149, 153, 164, American Express: page 67 (top), Camera Press: pages 138 (top & middle), 139 (bottom), J Allan Cash: pages 63, 163, Central Office of Information, London: page 25, Central Press Photo Ltd: page 139 (left), Chris Davis/Network: pages 21 (middle), 138 (bottom), James Davis Photography: page 63, Department of Health and Social Security: page 41, Humphrey Dobinson: pages 130, 142 (top), Henry Grant: pages 95, 107, Brian Hale: pages 28, 106, 111, 115, Barbara Hartley: pages 21 (right) (top), 53, IBM: page 91, Keystone Press Agency: pages 1, 139 (right), Frank Lane Agency: pages 77 (bottom), 142 (bottom), London Transport: page 27, Midland Bank: pages 125, 126, 127, Nelson Visual Resources Unit: pages 59, 61, 72, 82, 96, 97, 99, 118, 135, Peter Newarks Western Americana: page 63, Judah Passon/Network: pages 109, 121 (bottom), 139 (bottom right), The Post Office: pages 124, 125, David Pront: pages 98, 118, Ribble Motor Services Ltd: page 54, Rogue Images: page 21 (bottom), Safeway: page 81, S & G Press Agency Ltd: page 77 (top), Ronald Sheridan's Photo Library: page 7, Martin Smith: page 17, John Sturrock/Network: pages 121 (top), 122, 139 (bottom right), Bob Watson: pages 34, 74 76, Val Wilmer: page 150.

Diane Butler (pp. 5, 19, 22, 32, 62); Bob Harvey (pp. 9, 11, 12, 14, 15, 46, 47, 48, 57, 58, 70, 78, 97, 128, 154, 155); Peter Joyce (pp. 3, 4, 6, 7, 8, 9, 10, 12, 29, 37, 43, 44, 49, 51, 56, 58, 59, 66, 68, 71, 82, 94, 98, 99, 102, 104, 108, 111, 114, 117, 129, 131, 132, 134, 143, 144, 146, 148); Barrie Thorpe (pp. 30, 31, 50, 79, 81, 152, 156, 158, 161).

Filmset in Univers by Filmtype Services Limited, Scarborough, North Yorkshire.